THE

☆ STAR ☆
SPANGLED
Quote
Book

Bob Phillips

HARVEST HOUSE PUBLISHERS
Eugene, Oregon 97402

Verses marked KJV are taken from the King James Version of the Bible.

Cover design by Terry Dugan Design, Minneapolis, Minneasota

THE STAR-SPANGLED QUOTE BOOK

Copyright © 1997 by Bob Phillips
Published by Harvest House Publishers
Eugene, Oregon 97402

Library of Congress Cataloging-in-Publication Data

Phillips, Bob, 1940–
      The star-spangled quote book / Bob Phillips.
            p.   cm.
      ISBN 1-56507-725-3
      1. Quotations, English.   I. Title.
    PN6081.P485   1997   97-25719
    082—dc21   CIP

Printed in the United States of America.

97 98 99 00 01 02 / BP / 10 9 8 7 6 5 4 3 2 1

CONTENTS

☆ **A–Z** ☆

ABILITY

To do all that one is able to do is to be a man; to do all that one would like to do is to be a god.

Napoleon Bonaparte

ABORTION

Abortion is a skillfully marketed product sold to a woman at a crisis time in her life. If the product is defective, she can't return it for a refund.

Carol Everett

A woman who intentionally destroys a fetus is guilty of murder. And we do not even talk about the fine distinction as to its being completely formed or unformed.

Basil the Great

Abortion is advocated only by persons who have themselves been born.

Ronald Reagan

ABSENT

The absent always bear the blame.

The absent are always in the wrong.

The absent are like children, helpless
to defend themselves.

Charles Reade

Greater things are believed of those
who are absent.

Tacitus

The absent are never without fault. Nor the
present without excuse.

Benjamin Franklin

ABSTINENCE

The only way for a rich man to be healthy is by
exercise and abstinence, to live as if he were poor.

William Temple

ABSURDITY

It is the height of absurdity to sow little but weeds
in the first half of one's lifetime and expect to
harvest a valuable crop in the second half.

Percy Johnston

ACCEPTANCE

Acceptance of what has happened is the first
step to overcoming the consequences of
any misfortune.

William James

Gladly accept the gifts of the
present hour.

Horace

Acceptance says, True, this is my situation at the
moment. I'll look unblinkingly at the reality of it.
But I'll also open my hands to accept willingly
whatever a loving Father sends me.

Catherine Marshall

There is only one way to happiness, and that is to
cease worrying about things which are beyond
the power of our will.

Epictetus

You can't fight the desert . . . you
have to ride with it.

Louis L'Amour

Because you're not what I would have you be, I
blind myself to who, in truth, you are.

Madeline L'Engle

I am always content with what happens;
for I know that what God chooses is better
than what I choose.

Epictetus

What can't be cured, must be endured.

ACCOMPLISHMENT

Every worthwhile accomplishment, big
or little, has its stages of drudgery and
triumph: a beginning, a struggle,
and a victory.

We rate ability in men by what they finish,
not by what they begin.

Accomplishment will prove to be a journey,
not a destination.

Dwight D. Eisenhower

Always there will be, along the sidelines of life,
inferior souls who throw mud at those whose
attainments they do not quite understand. The man
who really accomplishes doesn't pay attention to
such detractors. If he did, he'd be on their level. He
keeps an eye singled on the higher goal—and the
mud never touches him.

Jerome P. Fleishman

ACCURACY

Accuracy is the twin brother of honesty;
inaccuracy, of dishonesty.

Charles Simmons

ACCUSATIONS

Even doubtful accusations leave a stain
behind them.

Thomas Fuller

ACHES AND PAINS

Aches and pains are your body's way of telling you something. And have you ever noticed that your body becomes more and more talkative as you grow older?

ACHIEVEMENT

Four steps to achievement: plan purposefully, prepare prayerfully, proceed positively, pursue persistently.

William A. Ward

It is not the critic who counts, not the man who points out how the strong man stumbles or where the doer of deeds could have done them better. The credit belongs to the man who is actually in the arena, whose face is marred by dust and sweat and blood; who strives valiantly; who errs and comes short again; who knows the great enthusiasms, the great devotions, and spends himself in a worthy cause; who at best knows the triumph of high achievement; and who, at the worst, if he fails, at least fails while daring greatly, so that his place shall never be with those cold and timid souls who know neither victory or defeat.

Theodore Roosevelt

It isn't the incompetent who destroy an organization. The incompetent never get in a position to destroy it. It is those who have achieved something and want to rest upon their achievements who are forever clogging things up.

F. M. Young

ACTION

Thought is the blossom; language the bud;
action the fruit behind it.

Ralph Waldo Emerson

Sooner begun, sooner done.

Be content to act, and leave the talking to others.

Baltasar Gracian

The individual activity of one man with backbone
will do more than a thousand men with a
mere wishbone.

William J.H. Boetcker

People avoid action often because they are afraid
of the consequences, for action means risk and
danger. Danger seems terrible from a distance; it
is not so bad if you have a close look at it. And
often it is a pleasant companion, adding to the
zest and delight of life.

Jawaharlal Nehru

Action springs not from thought, but from a
readiness for responsibility.

Dietrich Bonhoeffer

Thunder is good, thunder is impressive; but
it is the lightning that does the work.

Mark Twain

Action is eloquence.

Shakespeare

All the good maxims have been written. It only remains to put them into practice.

Blaise Pascal

Remember that the faith that removes mountains always carries a pick.

I have never heard anything about the resolutions of the apostles, but a great deal about their acts.

Horace Mann

Well done is better than well said.

Benjamin Franklin

I think there is something more important than believing: Action! The world is full of dreamers; there aren't enough who will move ahead and begin to take concrete steps to actualize their vision.

W. Clement Stone

ACTIONS

The actions of men are the best interpreters of their thoughts.

John Locke

ACTIVITY

Our nature consists in motion; complete rest is death.

Blaise Pascal

When the days are too short, chances are you are living at your best.

Earl Nightingale

ADMIRE

We always admire the other fellow more after we have tried to do his job.

William C. Feather

ADOLESCENCE

Adolescence is a kind of emotional seasickness. Both are funny, but only in retrospect.

Arthur Koestler

ADULTERY

Whoso committeth adultery with a woman lacketh understanding: he that doeth it destroyeth his own soul.

Proverbs 6:32

ADULTS

The value of marriage is not that adults produce children, but that children produce adults.

Peter de Vries

ADVENTURE

You can't cross the sea merely by standing and staring at the water. Don't let yourself indulge in vain wishes.

Rabindranath Tagore

ADVERSITY

Stars may be seen from the bottom of a deep well when they cannot be discerned from the top of a mountain. So are many things learned in adversity which the prosperous man dreams not of.

Charles Haddon Spurgeon

Adversity is easier borne than prosperity forgot.

Prosperity doth best discover vice, but adversity doth best discover virtue.

Francis Bacon

Anyone who proposes to do good must not expect people to roll stones out of his way, but must accept his lot calmly if they roll a few more upon it.

Albert Schweitzer

Kites rise highest against the wind—not with it.

Winston Churchill

Adversity comes with instruction in its hand.

Adversity makes a man wise, not rich.

The brook would lose its song if we removed the rocks.

Prosperity is a great teacher; adversity is a greater. Possession pampers the mind; privation trains and strengthens it.

William Hazlitt

The good things of prosperity are to be wished; but the good things that belong to adversity are to be admired.

Seneca

Every horse thinks his own pack the heaviest.

Fuller

Prosperity is not a just scale; adversity is the only balance to weigh friends.

Plutarch

I would never have amounted to anything were it not for adversity. I was forced to come up the hard way.

J.C. Penney

The firmest friendships have been formed in mutual adversity, as iron is most strongly united by the fiercest flame.

Charles Caleb Colton

Adversity not only draws people together, but brings forth that beautiful inward friendship.

Soren Kierkegaard

Adversity is the first path to Truth.

Lord Byron

Sweet are the uses of adversity.

William Shakespeare

No rose without a thorn.

Adversity is another way to measure the greatness of individuals. I never had a crisis that didn't make me stronger.

Lou Holtz

A clay pot sitting in the sun will always be a clay pot. It has to go through the white heat of the furnace to become porcelain.

Mildred W. Struven

Times of general calamity and confusion have ever been productive of the greatest minds. The purest ore is produced from the hottest furnace, and the brightest thunderbolt is elicited from the darkest storms.

Charles Caleb Colton

ADVICE

Never give advice in a crowd.

Advice is a stranger; if welcome he stays for the night; if not welcome he returns home the same day.

If you want to get rid of somebody, just tell 'em something for their own good.

Frank McKinney (Kin) Hubbard

The true secret of giving advice, is after you have honestly given it, to be perfectly indifferent whether it is taken or not and never persist in trying to set people right.

Hannah Whiteall Smith

Most of us ask for advice when we know
the answer but want a different one.

Ivern Bell

ADVOCATE

The first duty of a wise advocate is to
convince his opponents that he understands
their arguments, and sympathizes with
their just feelings.

Samuel Taylor Coleridge

AFFLICTION

Affliction comes to us all not to make us sad, but
sober, not to make us sorry, but wise; not to make
us despondent, but by its darkness to refresh us,
as the night refreshes the day; not to impoverish,
but to enrich us, as the plow enriches the field; to
multiply our joy, as the seed, by planting, is multi-
plied a thousand-fold.

Henry Ward Beecher

Affliction, like the iron-smith,
shapes as it smites.

Christian Nestell Bovee

AGE

If wrinkles must be written upon our brows, let
them not be written upon the heart. The spirit
should never grow old.

James Garfield

The woman who tells her age is either too young to have anything to lose or too old to have anything to gain.

I refuse to admit I'm more than fifty-two, even if that does make my sons illegitimate.

Lady Astor

Age does not depend upon years, but upon temperament and health. Some men are born old, and some never grow so.

Tryon Edwards

AGGRESSION

The truth is often a terrible weapon of aggression. It is possible to lie, and even to murder, with the truth.

AGITATION

Those who profess to favor freedom, and yet depreciate agitation, are men who want rain without thunder and lightning. They want the ocean without the roar of its many waters.

Frederick Douglass

AGNOSTIC

An agnostic is a person who says that he knows nothing about God and, when you agree with him, he becomes angry.

An agnostic found himself in trouble, and a friend suggested he pray. "How can I pray when I do not know whether or not there is a God?" he asked. "If you are lost in the forest," his friend replied, "you do not wait until you find someone before shouting for help."

Dan Plies

AGREED

I have never in my life learned anything from any man who agreed with me.

Dudley Field Malone

ALONE

In Genesis it says that it is not good for a man to be alone, but sometimes it is a great relief.

John Barrymore

AMBITION

Ambition often puts men upon doing the meanest offices: so climbing is performed in the same posture as creeping.

Jonathan Swift

Most people would succeed in small things, if they were not troubled with great ambitions.

Henry Wadsworth Longfellow

Keep away from people who try to belittle your ambitions. Small people always do that, but the really great make you feel that you, too, can become great.

Samuel Langhorne Clemens

AMERICA

Let our object be our country, our whole country,
and nothing but our country. And, by the blessing
of God, may that country itself become a vast and
splendid monument, not of oppression and terror,
but of wisdom, of peace, and of liberty, upon
which the world may gaze with
admiration forever.

Daniel Webster

America is not a mere body of traders; it is a body
of free men. Our greatness is built upon our
freedom—is moral, not material. We have a great
ardor for gain; but we have a deep passion
for the rights of man.

Woodrow Wilson

I believe the major threats to our country come
from within, not from without. These threats are
a decline in religious conviction, decline in moral
character, decline in the quality of family life and
in our understanding of the principle of
personal responsibility.

George Romney

I am certain that however great the hardships
and the trials which loom ahead, our America
will endure and the cause of human freedom
will triumph.

Cordell Hull

America is like a gigantic boiler. Once the fuse
is lighted under it, there is no limit to the
power it can generate.

Winston Churchill

What's right about America is that
although we have a mess of problems,
we have great capacity—intellect and
resources—to do something about them.

Henry Ford II

America's beauty is not only in its features;
its beauty is in the character underneath
those features.

Luci Swindoll

AMERICANS

An American is one who will sacrifice
property, ease and security in order that
he and his children may retain the rights
of free men.

Harold Le Claire Ickes

Cut an American into a hundred pieces
and boil him down, you will find him
all Fourth of July.

Wendell Phillips

I was born an American: I will live an American;
I shall die an American; and I intend to perform
the duties incumbent upon me in that character
to the end of my career. I mean to do this, with
absolute disregard of personal consequences.
What are personal consequences? What is the
individual man, with all the good or evil that may
betide him, in comparison with the good or evil
which may befall a great country in a crisis like
this, and in the midst of great transactions which
concern that country's fate? Let the consequences
be what will, I am careless.

No man can suffer too much, and no man can fall too soon, if he suffers or if he falls in defense of the liberties and Constitution of his country.

Daniel Webster

AMUSE

Be sincere. Be simple in words, manners and gestures. Amuse as well as instruct. If you can make a man laugh, you can make him think and make him like and believe you.

Alfred Emanuel Smith

ANCIENT TIMES

Let others praise ancient times; I am glad I was born in these.

Ovid

ANGER

He best keeps from anger who remembers that God is always looking upon him.

Plato

He that is slow to anger is better than the mighty; and he that ruleth his spirit than he that taketh a city.

Proverbs 16:32

He who conquers his anger has conquered an enemy.

If you are patient in one moment of anger, you will escape a hundred days of sorrow.

There is nothing more galling to angry people than the coolness of those on whom they wish to vent their spleen.

Alexandre Dumas

Two things at which a man should never be angry: what he can help, and what he cannot help.

He that would be angry and sin not, must not be angry with anything but sin.

Thomas Secker

Frequent fits of anger produce in the soul a propensity to be angry; which ofttimes ends in choler, bitterness, and morosity, when the mind becomes ulcerated, peevish, and querulous, and is wounded by the least occurrence.

Plutarch

To be angry is to revenge the faults of others on ourselves.

Alexander Pope

The intoxication of anger, like that of the grape, shows us to others, but hides us from ourselves. We injure our own cause in the opinion of the world when we too passionately defend it.

Charles Caleb Colton

Anger begins with folly, and ends with repentance.

H. G. Bohn

ANGRY

When a man is wrong and won't admit it,
he always gets angry.

Haliburton

ANGUISH

Anguish of mind has driven thousands to suicide,
anguish of body, none. This proves that the health
of the mind is of far more consequence to our
happiness than the health of the body, although
both are deserving of much more attention than
either of them receives.

ANTAGONIST

He that wrestles with us, strengthens our
nerves, and sharpens our skill. Our
antagonist is our helper.

Edmund Burke

ANTICIPATION

Nothing is so wretched or foolish as to anticipate
misfortunes. What madness is it to be expecting
evil before it comes.

Seneca

If pleasures are greatest in anticipation, just
remember that this is also true of trouble.

Elbert Hubbard

ANXIETY

Anxiety is a thin stream of fear trickling through
the mind. If encouraged, it cuts a channel into
which all other thoughts are drained.

Arthur Somers Roche

The thinner the ice, the more anxious is
everyone to see whether it will bear.

Josh Billings

APPLAUSE

When someone does something good,
applaud! You will make two
people happy.

Samuel Goldwyn

APPRECIATION

A word or a nod from the good has more
weight than the eloquent
speeches of others.

Plutarch

APPROVAL

I have yet to find the man, however
exalted his station, who did not do
better work and put forth greater effort under
a spirit of approval than under
a spirit of criticism.

Charles Schwab

ARBITRATION

Four out of five potential litigants will settle their disputes the first day they come together, if you will put the idea of arbitration into their heads.

Moses Henry Grossman

ASSOCIATES

Associate yourself with men of good quality if you esteem your own reputation, for 'tis better to be alone than in bad company.

George Washington

If you always live with those who are lame, you will yourself learn to limp.

He who has taken the bear into the boat must cross over with him.

ASSUMPTIONS

All miscommunication is the result of differing assumptions.

ATHEISM

To be an atheist requires an infinitely greater measure of faith than to receive all the great truths which atheism would deny.

Joseph Addison

The three great apostles of practical atheism that make converts without persecuting, and retain them without preaching, are health, wealth, and power.

Charles Caleb Colton

ATTACKING

Attacking is the only secret. Dare and the world always yields; or if it beats you sometimes, dare it again, and it will succumb.

William Makepeace Thackeray

ATTENTION

People who come with problems don't want solutions—they want attention.

ATTITUDE

Man is only miserable so far as he thinks himself so.

Jacopo Sannazaro

Occasions do not make a man either strong or weak, but they show what he is.

Thomas à Kempis

Nothing can work me damage except myself. The harm that I sustain I carry about with me, and am never a real sufferer but by my own fault.

Bernard of Clairvaux

A perverse and fretful disposition makes
any state of life unhappy.

Cicero

No life is so hard that you can't make it
easier by the way you take it.

Ellen Glasgow

It is not he who gives abuse that affronts,
but the view that we take of it as insulting; so
that when one provokes you it is your own
opinion which is provoking.

Epictetus

What is the difference between an
obstacle and an opportunity? Our attitude toward
it. Every opportunity has difficulty and every
difficulty has an opportunity.

J. Sidlow Baxter

We sing "Make a Joyful Noise Unto the Lord"
while our faces reflect the sadness of one who
has just buried a rich aunt who left everything
to her pregnant hamster.

Erma Bombeck

True wisdom lies in gathering the
precious things out of each day
as it goes by.

E. S. Bouton

Sunshine is delicious, rain is refreshing, wind
braces us up, snow is exhilarating; there is really
no such thing as bad weather, only different
kinds of good weather.

John Ruskin

Arrange whatever pieces come your way.

Virginia Woolf

It is no use to grumble and complain;
It's just as cheap and easy to rejoice;
When God sorts out the weather
and sends rain—
Why, rain's my choice.

James Whitcomb Riley

No man is happy unless he
believes he is.

Publilius Syrus

A man's as miserable as he thinks he is.

Marcus Annaeus Seneca

When work is a pleasure, life is a joy! When
work is a duty, life is slavery.

Maxim Gorky

When a dog runs at you, whistle for him.

Henry David Thoreau

Life is 10 percent what you make it, and
90 percent how you take it.

Irving Berlin

I wept because I had no shoes, until I saw
a man who had no feet.

It is our relation to circumstances that
determines their influence over us. The same
wind that carries one vessel into port may
blow another off shore.

Christian Bovee

What you can't get out of, get into
wholeheartedly.

Mignon McLaughlin

He that is discontented in one place will
seldom be happy in another.

Aesop

The really happy man is one who can
enjoy the scenery on a detour.

There is no banquet but some dislike
something in it.

Thomas Fuller

If the sky falls, we shall catch larks.

Since the house is on fire let us
warm ourselves.

I don't think of all the misery, but of all the
beauty that still remains.

Anne Frank

He shall fare well who confronts
circumstances aright.

Plutarch

The art of life is to know how to enjoy a
little and to endure much.

William Hazlitt.

The sparrow flying to the rear of the hawk
thinks the hawk is fleeing.

I have resolved that from this day on, I will
do all the business I can honestly, have all the
fun I can reasonably, do all the good I
can willingly, and save my digestion
by thinking pleasantly.

Robert Louis Stevenson

Most folks are about as happy as they
make up their minds to be.

Abraham Lincoln

We are not troubled by things, but by the
opinion which we have of things.

Epictetus

It may not be your fault for being down, but
it's got to be your fault for not
getting up.

Steve Davis

Don't curse the darkness—light a candle.

If you have arthritis, calmly say,
I was always complaining about the
ruts in the road until I realized that
the ruts are the road.

AUTHOR

The two most engaging powers of an author are to make new things familiar, and familiar things new.

Samuel Johnson

AVOIDANCE

We run away all the time to avoid coming face to face with ourselves.

BABIES

Babies are such a nice way to start people.

Don Herold

Kissing the baby touches the loving parent.

BAD

No man ever became thoroughly bad all at once.

If you would be good, first believe you are bad.

Epictetus

BATTLE

You may have to fight a battle more than once to win it.

Margaret Thatcher

BEACH

A beach is a place where people slap
you on the back and ask how
you're peeling.

BEAUTY

No one can live on beauty, but they
can die for it.

Think of all the beauty still left around
you and be happy.

Anne Frank

I think women see me on the cover of
magazines and think I never have a pimple or
bags under my eyes. You have to realize that's
after two hours of hair and makeup, plus
retouching. Even I don't wake up looking
like Cindy Crawford.

Cindy Crawford

BEGINNING

A road of a thousand miles
begins with one step.

He who is outside the door has already a
good part of his journey behind him.

The beginning is half of every action.

More powerful than the will to win is
the courage to begin.

BEHAVIOR

Behavior is a mirror in which every one
displays his image.

Johann Wolfgang von Goethe

We create our fate every day . . . most of
the ills we suffer from are directly traceable
to our own behavior.

Henry Miller

If you want to change attitudes, start with
a change in behavior.

William Glasser

BEING A MAN

A man shares his days with hunger, thirst, and
cold, with the good times and the bad, and the
first part of being a man is to understand that.

Louis L'Amour

BELLY

He who does not mind his belly will hardly
mind anything else.

Samuel Johnson

BENEVOLENCE

I never knew a child of God being bankrupted by
his benevolence. What we keep we may lose, but
what we give to Christ we are sure to keep.

Theodore Ledyard Cuyler

BEST

I have never had a policy; I have simply
tried to do what seemed best each day,
as each day came.

Abraham Lincoln

Any man's life will be filled with constant and unexpected encouragement if he makes up his mind
to do his level best each day.

Booker T. Washington

I do the very best I know how—the very best I
can; and I mean to keep on doing so until the end.

Abraham Lincoln

On God for all events depend;
You cannot want when God's your friend.
Weigh well your part and do your best;
Leave to your Maker all the rest.

Nathaniel Cotton

Good, better, best; never rest till "good" be
"better" and "better," best.

Mother Goose

BIBLE

It is impossible to enslave, mentally or socially, a
Bible reading people. The principles of the Bible
are the groundwork of human freedom.

Horace Greeley

The best evidence that the Bible is the inspired word of God is to be found within its covers. It proves itself.

Charles Hodge

I have made it a practice for several years to read the Bible in the course of every year.

John Quincy Adams

All that I am I owe to Jesus Christ, revealed to me in His divine Book.

David Livingstone

I thoroughly believe in a university education for both men and women, but I believe a knowledge of the Bible without a college course is more valuable than a college course without a knowledge of the Bible.

Billy Graham

The book to read is not the one which thinks for you, but the one which makes you think. No book in the world equals the Bible for that.

James McCosh

No man ever did, or ever will become most truly eloquent without being a constant reader of the Bible, and an admirer of the purity and sublimity of its language.

Fisher Ames

It was the Lord who put into my mind
(I could feel His hand upon me) the fact that
it would be possible to sail from here to the
Indies. All who heard of my project rejected
it with laughter, ridiculing me. There is no
question that the inspiration was from the
Holy Spirit, because He comforted me
with rays of marvelous inspiration from the
Holy Scriptures.

Christopher Columbus

When you have read the Bible, you will know
it is the word of God, because you will have
found it the key to your own heart, your own
happiness and your own duty.

(Thomas) Woodrow Wilson

The Bible is one of the greatest blessings
bestowed by God on the children of men. It
has God for its author, salvation for its end,
and truth without any mixture for its matter. It
is all pure, all sincere; nothing too much;
nothing wanting.

John Locke

Read Demosthenes or Cicero; read Plato, Aristotle, or any others of that class; I grant you that you will be attracted, delighted, moved, enraptured by them in a surprising manner; but if, after reading them, you turn to the perusal of the sacred volume, whether you are willing or unwilling, it will affect you so powerfully, it will so penetrate your heart, and impress itself so strangely on your mind that, compared with its energetic influence, the beauties of rhetoricians and philosophers will almost entirely disappear; so that it is easy to perceive something divine in the sacred Scriptures, which far surpasses the highest attainments and ornaments of human industry.

John Calvin

So great is my veneration for the Bible, that the earlier my children begin to read it the more confident will be my hopes that they will prove useful citizens to their country and respectable members of society.

John Quincy Adams

I speak as a man of the world to men of the world; and I say to you, search the Scriptures! The Bible is the book of all others, to be read at all ages, and in all conditions of human life; not to be read once or twice or thrice through, and then laid aside, but to be read in small portions of one or two chapters every day, and never to be intermitted, unless by some overruling necessity.

John Quincy Adams

The Bible is God's chart for you to steer by, to keep you from the bottom of the sea, and to show you where the harbor is, and how to reach it without running on rocks or bars.

Henry Ward Beecher

BIGOTRY

How it infuriates a bigot, when he is forced to drag into the light his dark convictions.

Logan Pearsall Smith

BILLBOARD

I think that I shall never see
A billboard lovely as a tree.
Indeed, unless the billboards fall
I'll never see a tree at all.

Ogden Nash

BITE

The proverb warns that "you should not bite the hand that feeds you." But maybe you should, if it prevents you from feeding
yourself.

Thomas Szasz

BLAME

When you blame others, you give up your power to change.

BLARNEY

Baloney is the unvarnished lie laid on so thick you hate it. Blarney is flattery laid on so thin you love it.

Bishop Fulton J. Sheen

BLESSINGS

Reflect upon your present blessings, of which every man has many, not on your past misfortunes, of which all men have some.

Charles John Huffam Dickens

BLIND EYE

Every man needs a blind eye and a deaf ear, so when people applaud, you'll only hear half of it, and when people salute, you'll only see part of it. Believe only half the praise and half the criticism.

Charles Spurgeon

BLUFF

The hardest tumble a man can make is to fall over his own bluff.

Ambrose Gwinnett Bierce

BOAST

Don't place too much confidence in a man
who boasts of being as honest as the day is long.
Wait until you meet him at night.

Robert Chambers (Bob) Edwards

With all his tumid boasts, he's like the
swordfish, who only wears his weapon
in his mouth.

Samuel Madden

BOATMEN

Too many boatmen will row the boat up
the mountain.

BODY LANGUAGE

Look in the face of the person to whom you are
speaking if you wish to know his real sentiments,
for he can command his words more easily
than his countenance.

Lord Chesterfield

BOLD

Avoiding danger is no safer in the long run
than outright exposure. The fearful are caught
as often as the bold.

Helen Keller

BOLDNESS

When you cannot make up your mind which of
two evenly balanced courses of action you
should take—choose the bolder.

W. J. Slim

Don't be afraid to take a big step if one is
indicated. You can't cross a chasm in two
small jumps.

David Lloyd George

In difficult situations, when hope seems
feeble, the boldest plans are safest.

Titus Livy

Put a grain of boldness into
everything you do.

Baltasar Gracian

I hate to see things done by halves.
If it be right, do it boldly; if it be
wrong, leave it undone.

Bernard Gilpin

BOOK

Everything comes to him who waits.
Except a loaned book.

Frank McKinney (Kin) Hubbard

BOOKS

When I get a little money, I buy books; and
if any is left, I buy food and clothes.

Erasmus

Books are embalmed minds.

Christian Nestell Bovee

He that loves not books before he comes to thirty years of age, will hardly love them enough afterward to understand them.

Edward Hyde

A house without books is like a room without windows. No man has a right to bring up his children without surrounding them with books, if he has the means to buy them. It is a wrong to his family. Children learn to read by being in the presence of books. The love of knowledge comes with reading and grows upon it. And the love of knowledge, in a young mind, is almost a warrant against the inferior excitement of passions and vices.

Horace Mann

There is more treasure in books than in all the pirates' loot on Treasure Island . . . and best of all, you can enjoy these riches every day of your life.

Walt Disney

Read the best books first, or you may not have a chance to read them all.

Henry David Thoreau

BORE

A healthy male adult bore consumes each year one and a half times his own weight in other people's patience.

John Updike

The secret of being a bore is to
tell everything.

Voltaire

BORROWING

When I lent, I was a friend; and when I
asked, I was unkind.

The borrower is servant to the lender.

Proverbs 22:7

He who borrows sells his freedom.

He who is quick at borrowing, is
slow in paying.

BOSS

If thou art a master, be sometimes blind; if a
servant, sometimes deaf.

Thomas Fuller

The eye of the master will do more work than
both of his hands: not to oversee workmen,
is to leave your purse open.

Benjamin Franklin

BOUND

I am not bound to win,
but I am bound to be true.
I am not bound to succeed,
but I am bound to live up to what light I have.

Abraham Lincoln

BRAIN

The biggest human brain on record was that of an idiot; one of the smallest was that of the gifted French writer Anatole France.

Ashley Montagu

BRAVERY

Every dog is valiant at his own door.

BREVITY

Brevity is the best recommendation of speech, whether in a senator or an orator.

Cicero

BROKEN HEART

All are not merry that dance lightly.

BUCKET

Don't throw away the old bucket until you know whether the new one holds water.

BUILDING

My precept to all who build is that the owner should be an ornament to the house, and not the house to the owner.

Cicero

He that is fond of building will soon ruin
himself without the help of enemies.

Plutarch

BULLY

A bully is always a coward.

BUNGEE JUMPING

Whoever invented bungee jumping must have
watched a lot of Road Runner cartoons.

Nick Arnette

BURDEN

A burden of one's own choice is not felt.

It has been well said that no man ever sank under
the burden of the day. It is when
tomorrow's burden is added to the burden
of today that the weight is more than a
man can bear.

George Macdonald

Pray not for lighter burdens, but for
stronger backs.

Theodore Roosevelt

BUSINESS

Business is like a wheelbarrow: Nothing ever
happens until you start pushing.

Business is like riding a bicycle: Either you keep moving or you fall down.

John David Wright

To establish a business is easy; to maintain it, difficult.

Half the time men think they are talking business, they are wasting time.

E. W. Howe

BUSY

To be busy is man's only happiness.

Mark Twain

BUT

Oh, now comes that bitter word — "but," which makes all nothing that was said before, that smooths and wounds, that strikes and dashes more than a flat denial, or a plain disgrace.

Samuel Daniel

BUYER

The buyer needs a hundred eyes, the seller but one.

Caveat emptor—let the buyer beware.

CAB

Cab drivers are living proof that practice
does not make perfect.

Howard Ogden

CALAMITY

He who forsees calamities suffers
them twice over.

Beilby Porteous

Calamity is the perfect glass wherein we
truly see and know ourselves.

Sir William Davenant

CALM

They sicken of the calm,
who know the storm.

Dorothy Parker

CAMPFIRE

What a friendly and companionable thing is a campfire! How generous and outright it is! It plays for you when you wish to be lively, and it glows for you when you wish to be reflective.

David Grayson

CANDOR

All faults may be forgiven of him who has perfect candor.

Walt Whitman

CANOE

Every man paddles his own canoe.

Frederick Marryat

CAN'T

Knock the "t" off the "can't."

George Reeves

CAPITALISM

Capitalism and communism stand at opposite poles. Their essential difference is this: The communist, seeing the rich and his fine home says: "No man should have so much." The capitalist, seeing the same thing, says: "All men should have as much."

Phelps Adams

CAPTAINS

Too many captains run the ship aground.

CAR ALARM

They erupt like indignant metal jungle birds, and they whoop all night. They make American cities sound like lunatic rain forests, all the wildlife affrighted, violated, outraged, shrieking . . . In a neighborhood of apartment buildings, one such beast rouses sleepers by the hundreds, even thousands. They wake, roll over, moan, jam pillows on their ears and try to suppress the adrenaline. Car thieves, however, pay no attention to the noise.

Lance Morrow

CARE

(Cast) all your care upon Him; for He careth for you.

1 Peter 5:7

CAREER

To find a career to which you are adapted by nature, and then to work hard at it, is about as near to a formula for success and happiness as the world provides.

Mark Sullivan

CAUTION

The chief danger in life is that you may take too many precautions.

Alfred Adler

CELEBRITY

The nice thing about being a celebrity is that when you bore people, they think it's their fault.

Henry Kissinger

CHALLENGE

We gain nothing by being with such as ourselves: we encourage each other in mediocrity. I am always longing to be with men more excellent than myself.

Charles Lamb

CHANGE

A change is as good as a rest.

Changing of works is lighting of hearts.

A new broom sweeps clean.

If we lose touch with the river of change and enter a backwater, become self-centered and self-satisfied, and ostrichlike ignore what happens elsewhere, we do so at our peril.

Jawaharlal Nehru

The only time a woman really succeeds in changing a man is when he's a baby.

Natalie Wood

If you want to make enemies, try to change something.

Woodrow Wilson

Everything changes continually. What is history, indeed, but a record of change? And if there had been very few changes in the past, there would have been little of history to write.

Jawaharlal Nehru

Nothing in the world that is alive remains unchanging. All nature changes from day to day and minute to minute; only the dead stop growing and are quiescent. Fresh water runs on, and if you stop it, it becomes stagnant. So also is it with the life of man and the life of a nation.

Jawaharlal Nehru

In prosperity prepare for a change; in adversity hope for one.

James Burgh

Nothing is permanent but change.

Heraclitus

The absurd man is he who never changes.

Auguste Barthelemy

Nobody told me how hard and lonely change is.

Joan Gilbertson

The world hates change, yet it is the only thing that has brought progress.

Charles F. Kettering

When you're through changing, you're through.

Bruce Barton

With me a change of trouble is as good as a vacation.

William Lloyd George

Innovation is resisted by individuals who are unwilling to risk the status they have achieved and jealously guard their own job against any change.

William T. Brady

All change represents loss of some kind; that's why some of us resist it so strongly.

There is a certain relief in change, even though it be from bad to worse.

Washington Irving

All is change; all yields its place and goes.

Euripides

All changes, even the most longed for, have their melancholy; for what we leave behind us is a part of ourselves; we must die to one life before we can enter into another.

Anatole France

We are restless because of incessant change, but we would be frightened if change were stopped.

Lyman Lloyd Bryson

After you've done a thing the same way for two years, look it over carefully. After five years, look at it with suspicion. And after ten years, throw it away and start all over.

Alfred Edward Perlman

Change is the law of life, and those who look only to the past or the present are certain to miss the future.

John F. Kennedy

People are afraid of the future, of the unknown. If a man faces up to it, and takes the dare of the future, he can have some control over his destiny. That's an exciting idea to me—better than waiting with everybody else to see what's going to happen.

John Glenn

Everything flows, nothing stays still.

Heraclitus

One must change one's tactics every ten years if one wishes to maintain one's superiority.

Napoleon Bonaparte

Just when I think I have learned the way to live, life changes.

Hugh Prather

Change is what people fear most.

Fyodor Dostoyevsky

Everyone thinks of changing the world, but no one thinks of changing himself.

Leo Tolstoi

CHARACTER

A man never discloses his own character so clearly as when he describes another's.

Jean Paul Richter

Be more concerned with your character than with your reputation. Your character is what you really are while your reputation is merely what others think you are.

John Wooden

Slander cannot make a good man bad; when the water recedes the stone is still there.

Character builds slowly, but it can be torn down with incredible swiftness.

Faith Baldwin

Character is made by what you stand for; reputation by what you fall for.

Alexander Woollcott

Talents are best nurtured in solitude; character is best formed in the stormy billows of the world.

Johann Wolfgang von Goethe

A man of character will make himself worthy of any position he is given.

Mahatma Gandhi

A dwarf is small, even if he stands on a mountain; a collossus keeps his height, even if he stands in a well.

Seneca

A sound body is a first-class thing; a sound mind is an even better thing; but the thing that counts for most in the individual, as in the nation, is character, the sum of those qualities which make a man a good man and a woman a good woman.

Theodore Roosevelt

A good name lost is seldom regained. When character is gone, all is gone, and one of the richest jewels of life is lost forever.

Joel Hawes

I have found some of the best reasons I ever had for remaining at the bottom simply by looking at the men at the top.

Frank Moore Colby

He who acts wickedly in private life can never be expected to show himself noble in public conduct. He that is base at home will not acquit himself with honor abroad; for it is not the man, but only the place, that is changed.

Aeschines

A man's character is the reality of himself. His reputation is the opinion others have formed of him. Character is in him; reputation is from other people—that is the substance, this is the shadow.

Henry Ward Beecher

The best advertisement of a workshop is first-class work. The strongest attraction to Christianity is a well-made Christian character.

Theodore Ledyard Cuyler

A good anvil does not fear the hammer.

CHARITY

The best thing to give to your enemy is forgiveness; to an opponent, tolerance; to a friend, your heart; to your child, a good example; to a father, deference; to your mother, conduct that will make her proud of you; to yourself, respect; to all men, charity.

Francis Maitland Balfour

Though I speak with the tongues of men and of angels, and have not charity, I am become as sounding brass, or a tinkling cymbal. ·

1 Corinthians 13:1-3

If you haven't any charity in your heart, you have the worst kind of heart trouble.

Bob Hope

CHARM

The basic thing which contributes to charm is the ability to forget oneself and be engrossed in other people.

Eleanor Roosevelt

CHASE

With the catching ends the pleasures of the chase.

Abraham Lincoln

CHEATING

He that will cheat at play, will cheat
you any way.

I have found that if a young person cheats in
school he has a tendency to cheat in life. It starts
a trend as he begins to harden his heart and this
becomes a terrible danger.

Billy Graham

CHEER

The best way to cheer yourself is to try to
cheer somebody else up.

Mark Twain

Every one must have felt that a cheerful friend is
like a sunny day, which sheds its brightness on all
around; and most of us can, as we choose, make
of this world either a palace or a prison.

Sir John Lubbock

A cheerful temper joined with innocence will make
beauty attractive, knowledge delightful, and wit
good-natured. It will lighten sickness, poverty,
and affliction; convert ignorance into
an amiable simplicity, and render
deformity itself agreeable.

Joseph Addison

The cheerful live longest in years, and afterwards
in our regards. Cheerfulness is the offshoot
of goodness.

Christian Nestell Bovee

Wondrous is the strength of cheerfulness,
and its power of endurance—the cheerful man
will do more in the same time, will do it better,
will persevere in it longer, than the
sad or sullen.

Thomas Carlyle

The true source of cheerfulness is benevolence.
The soul that perpetually overflows with kindness
and sympathy will always be cheerful.

Parke Godwin

Cheerfulness is like money well-expended in
charity; the more we dispense of it, the
greater our possession.

Victor Hugo

CHILDREN

First you teach a child to talk; then you have
to teach it to be quiet.

There never was child so lovely but his mother
was glad to get him asleep.

Ralph Waldo Emerson

If a child annoys you, quiet him by brushing
his hair. If this doesn't work, use the
other side of the brush on the other
end of the child.

Don't threaten a child; either punish him
or forgive him.

Talmud

There's only one pretty child in the world,
and every mother has it.

Children today are tyrants. They contradict their parents, gobble their food, and tyrannize their teachers.

Socrates

In general my children refused to eat anything that hadn't danced on TV.

Erma Bombeck

Each day of our lives we make deposits in the memory banks of our children.

Charles R. Swindoll

Children require guidance and sympathy far more than instruction.

Anne Sullivan

He that has no children brings them up well.

It goes without saying that you should never have more children than you have car windows.

Erma Bombeck

Any kid will run an errand for you, if you ask him at bedtime.

Red Skelton

Children have never been very good at listening to their elders, but they have never failed to imitate them.

James Baldwin

Children are poor men's riches.

Let your children go if you want
to keep them.

Malcolm Forbes

Pretty much all the honest truth-telling there is
in the world is done by children.

Oliver Wendell Holmes

Lo, children are an heritage of the LORD: and
the fruit of the womb is his reward.

Psalms 127:3

Genuine appreciation of other people's
children is one of the rarer virtues.

Harlan Miller

The best smell is bread, the best savour salt,
the best love that of children.

Small children disturb your sleep;
big children, your life.

Children are natural mimics—they act like their
parents in spite of every attempt to teach
them good manners.

Nature kindly warps our judgment about our
children, especially when they are young,
when it would be a fatal thing for them
if we did not love them.

George Santayana

A little child weighs on your knee, a big
one on your heart.

CHRIST

The great mistake of my life has been that I tried
to be moral without faith in Jesus; but I have
learned that true morality can only keep pace with
trust in Christ as my Saviour.

Gerrit Smith

If Socrates would enter the room we should rise
and do him honor, but if Jesus Christ came into
the room we should fall down on our
knees and worship Him.

Napoleon Bonaparte

I search in vain in history to find the similar to
Jesus Christ, or anything which can approach the
gospel. Neither history, nor humanity, nor the
ages, nor nature, offer me anything with which I
am able to compare or explain it. There is nothing
there which is not beyond the march of events
and above the human mind. What happiness it
gives to those who believe it! What marvels there
which those admire who reflect upon it!

Napoleon Bonaparte

As the print of the seal on the wax is the
express image of the seal itself, so Christ
is the express image—the perfect
representation of God.

Ambrose of Milan

In his life, Christ is an example, showing us how to live; in his death, he is a sacrifice, satisfying for our sins; in his resurrection, a conqueror; in his ascension, a king; in his intercession, a high priest.

Martin Luther.

The sum of the whole matter is this, that our civilization cannot survive materially unless it be redeemed spiritually. It can be saved only by becoming permeated with the spirit of Christ and being made free and happy by the practices which spring out of that spirit.

Woodrow Wilson

CHRISTIAN

There is one single fact which we may oppose to all the wit and argument of infidelity, namely, that no man ever repented of being a Christian on his death-bed.

Hannah More

Going to church doesn't make you a Christian any more than going to a garage makes you an automobile.

William Ashley (Billy) Sunday

There never was found in any age of the world either philosopher or sect, or law, or discipline which did so highly exalt the public good as the Christian faith.

Francis Bacon

CHRISTIANITY

Christianity has not been tried and found wanting;
it has been found difficult and not tried.

Gilbert Keith Chesterton

Christianity everywhere gives dignity to labor,
sanctity to marriage, and brotherhood to man.
Where it may not convince, it enlightens; where it
does not convert, it restrains; where it does not
renew, it refines; where it does not sanctify, it
subdues and elevates. It is profitable alike for
this world, and for the world that is to come.

Sir George St. Patrick Lawrence

When a man is opposed to Christianity, it is
because Christianity is opposed to him. Your
infidel is usually a person who resents the
opposition of Christianity to that in his nature and
life which Jesus came to rebuke and destroy.

Robert Hall

Whatever men may think of religion, the historic
fact is that in proportion as the institutions of
Christianity lose their hold upon the multitudes,
the fabric of society is in peril.

Arthur Tappan Pierson

Christianity is the companion of liberty in all
its conflicts, the cradle of its infancy, and the
divine source of its claims.

Alexis de Tocqueville

The distinction between Christianity and all other systems of religion consists largely in this, that in these others men are found seeking after God, while Christianity is God seeking after men.

Thomas Arnold

Where science speaks of improvement, Christianity speaks of renovation; where science speaks of development, Christianity speaks of sanctification; where science speaks of progress, Christianity speaks of perfection.

Joseph Parrish Thompson

The real security of Christianity is to be found in its benevolent morality; in its exquisite adaption to the human heart; in the facility with which it accommodates itself to the capacity of every human intellect; in the consolation which it bears to every house of mourning; and in the light with which it brightens the great mystery of the grave.

Thomas Babington Macaulay

CITIZEN

The first requisite of a good citizen in this republic of ours is that he shall be able and willing to pull his weight.

Theodore Roosevelt

The true Christian is the true citizen, lofty of purpose, resolute in endeavor, ready for a hero's deeds, but never looking down on his task because it is cast in the day of small things; scornful of baseness, awake to his own duties as well as to his rights, following the higher law with reverence, and in this world doing all that in his power lies, so that when death comes he may feel that mankind is in some degree better because he lived.

Theodore Roosevelt

CIVILIZATION

You can't say civilization isn't advancing; in every war they kill you in a new way.

Will Rogers

CIVILIZED

Anyone can be a barbarian; it requires a terrible effort to remain a civilized man.

Leonard Sidney Woolf

CLEVERNESS

The height of cleverness is to be able to conceal it.

Francois de la Rochefoucauld

What cleverness hides, cleverness will reveal.

COCKEYED

If you have one eye on yesterday, and one eye on tomorrow, you're going to be cockeyed today.

COLD

A bad cold wouldn't be so annoying if it weren't for the advice of our friends.

Frank McKinney (Kin) Hubbard

COMEDY

Comedy is in my blood. Frankly, I wish it were in my act!

Rodney Dangerfield

Comedy has to be truth. You take the truth and put a little curlicue at the end.

Sid Caesar

COMMUNICATION

Think like a wise man but communicate in the language of the people.

William Butler Yeats

Good communication is as stimulating as black coffee, and just as hard to sleep after.

Ann Morrow Lindbergh

COMPANION

Everybody's companion is nobody's friend.

COMPARISON

It is comparison that makes men
happy or miserable.

COMPLAINTS

If I were to attempt to answer all the criticisms and
complaints I receive, I would have no time for any
other business. From day to day I do the best I
can and will continue to do so till the end. If in the
end I come out all right, then the complaints and
criticisms and what is said against me will make
no difference. But, if the end brings me out wrong,
then 10 angels coming down from heaven to
swear I was right would still make no difference.

Abraham Lincoln

We have no more right to put our discordant
states of mind into the lives of those around us
and rob them of their sunshine and brightness
than we have to enter their houses and
steal their silverware.

Julia Moss Seton

CONDUCT

The reputation of a thousand years may be
determined by the conduct of one hour.

CONFERENCE

A conference is a gathering of important people
who singly can do nothing, but together can
decide that nothing can be done.

Fred Allen

No grand idea was ever born in a conference, but
a lot of foolish ideas have died there.

F. Scott Fitzgerald

CONFESSION

Confession is the first step to repentance.

He's half absolv'd who has confess'd.

Matthew Prior

Confession of our faults is the next
thing to innocence.

Publilius Syrus

A generous confession disarms slander.

Thomas Fuller

The confession of evil works is the first
beginning of good works.

Saint Augustine

CONFLICT

It is well to remind ourselves that anxiety
signifies a conflict, and so long as a conflict is
going on, a constructive solution is possible.

Rollo May

CONFRONTATION

Whatever you are trying to avoid won't go
away until you confront it.

CONFUSION

Times of general calamity and confusion have ever been productive of the greatest minds. The purest ore is produced from the hottest furnace, and the brightest thunderbolt is elicited from the darkest storms.

Charles Caleb Colton

CONSCIENCE

Cowardice asks, Is it safe? Expediency asks, Is it politic? Vanity asks, Is it popular? but Conscience asks, Is it right?

William Morley Punshon

Conscience, true as the needle to the pole, points steadily to the pole-star of God's eternal justice, reminding the soul of the fearful realities of the life to come.

Ezra Hall Gillett

It is astonishing how soon the whole conscience begins to unravel if a single stitch drops. One single sin indulged in makes a hole you could put your head through.

Charles Buxton

Our greatest happiness does not depend on the condition of life in which chance has placed us, but is always the result of a good conscience, good health, occupation, and freedom in all just pursuits.

Thomas Jefferson

The only tyrant I accept in this world is
the still voice within.

Mahatma Gandhi

He who sacrifices his conscience to ambition
burns a picture to obtain the ashes.

Conscience takes up more room than all the rest
of a person's insides.

Mark Twain

Preserve your conscience always soft and
sensitive. If but one sin forces its way into that
tender part of the soul and is suffered to dwell
there, the road is paved for
a thousand iniquities.

Isaac Watts

A good conscience makes an easy couch.

A clear conscience fears not false
accusations.

Conscience is the root of all true courage;
if a man would be brave, let him
obey his conscience.

James Freeman Clarke

CONTEMPT

Many can bear adversity, but few contempt.

CONTENTMENT

Who is rich? He that is content.
Who is that? Nobody.

Benjamin Franklin

Be content with such things as ye have.

Hebrews 13:5

He has nothing, who is not contented.

A contented mind is a continual feast.

There are nine requisites for contented living:
Health enough to make work a pleasure. Wealth
enough to support your needs. Strength to battle
with difficulties and overcome them. Grace
enough to confess your sins and forsake them.
Patience enough to toil until some good is
accomplished. Charity enough to see some
good in your neighbor. Love enough to move
you to be useful and helpful to others. Faith
enough to make real the things of God.
Hope enough to remove all anxious fears
concerning the future.

Johann von Goethe

To be glad of life, because it gives you the chance to love and to work and to play and to look up at the stars; to be satisfied with your possessions, but not contented with yourself until you have made the best of them; to despise nothing in the world except falsehood and meanness, and to fear nothing except cowardice; to be governed by your admirations rather than by your disgusts; to covet nothing that is your neighbor's except his kindness of heart and gentleness of manners; to think seldom of your enemies, often of your friends, and every day of Christ; and to spend as much time as you can, with body and with spirit, in God's out-of-doors—these are little guideposts on the footpath to peace.

Henry Van Dyke

Contentment with the divine will is the best remedy we can apply to misfortunes.

To be without some of the things you want is an indispensable part of happiness.

Bertrand Russell

The secret of contentment is knowing how to enjoy what you have, and to be able to lose all desire for things beyond your reach.

Lin Yutang

CONTRAST

The lustre of diamonds is invigorated by the inter-position of darker bodies; the lights of a picture are created by the shades.

CONVERSATION

For good or ill, your conversation is your advertisement. Every time you open your mouth you let men look into your mind. Do they see it well-clothed, neat, businesslike?

Bruce Barton

One reason why we find so few people rational and agreeable in conversation is that there is scarcely any one not rather thinking on what he is intending to say, than on answering exactly the question put to him. The cleverest and the most complaisant are satisfied if they only seem attentive, though we can discover in their eyes and distraction that they are wandering from what is addressed to them, and are impatient to return to what they were saying; whereas they should recollect that if they wish to please or convince others, they must no be overanxious to please themselves, and that to listen attentively, and to answer precisely, is the greatest perfection of conversion.

Francois de la Rochefoucauld

The first ingredient in conversation is truth; the next, good sense; the third, good humor; and the fourth, wit.

Sir William Temple

The world of conversationalists, in my experience, is divided into two classes: those who listen to what the other person has to say, and those who use the interval to plan their next remark.

Bruce Bliven

CONVICTION

Courage is more than standing for a firm conviction. It includes the risk of questioning that conviction.

Julian Weber Gordon

A "No" uttered from deepest conviction is better and greater than a "Yes" merely uttered to please, or what is worse, to avoid trouble.

Mahatma Gandhi

The height of your accomplishments will equal the depth of your convictions.

William F. Scolavino

COOKS

It is no wonder that diseases are innumerable: count the cooks.

Seneca

CORDLESS

Cordless phones are great. If you can find them.

Glenn Foster

COUNSEL

Give neither counsel nor salt till you are
asked for it.

Good counsel never comes too late.

COUNSELOR

A counselor is one who simply articulates
the human condition.

R. E. Phillips

Without wise leadership, a nation is in trouble; but
with good counselors there is safety.

Proverbs 11:14

COURAGE

We can never be certain of our courage till
we have faced danger.

Francois de La Rochefoucauld

Man cannot discover new oceans until he has
courage to lose sight of the shore.

Courage is being scared to death . . . and
saddling up anyway.

John Wayne

Be courageous! . . . I have seen many
depressions in business. Always America
has come out stronger and more prosperous.
Be as brave as your fathers before you.
Have faith! Go forward.

Thomas A. Edison

Courage is resistance to fear, mastery of fear—not absence of fear.

Mark Twain

God grant me the courage not to give up what I think is right, even though I think it is hopeless.

Admiral Chester W. Nimitz

On many of the great issues of our time, men have lacked wisdom because they have lacked courage.

William Benton

Last, but by no means least, courage—moral courage, the courage of one's convictions, the courage to see things through. The world is in a constant conspiracy against the brave. It's the age-old struggle—the roar of the crowd on one side and the voice of your conscience on the other.

Douglas Macarthur

There is nothing in the world so much admired as a man who knows how to bear unhappiness with courage.

Marcus Annaeus Seneca

One man with courage makes a majority.

He who loses wealth loses much; he who loses a friend loses more; but he who loses his courage loses all.

Miguel de Cervantes

Courage is the first of the human qualities
because it is the quality which guarantees
all the others.

Sir Winston Churchill

It is courage, courage, courage, that raises the
blood of life to crimson splendor.
Live bravely and present a brave
front to adversity!

Horace

The hallmark of courage in our age of conformity
is the capacity to stand on one's convictions—not
obstinately or defiantly (these are gestures of
defensiveness, not courage) nor as a gesture
of retaliation, but simply because these are
what one believes.

Rollo May

One doesn't discover new lands without
consenting to lose sight of the shore for a
very long time.

Andre Gide

Courage is fear holding on a minute longer.

General George S. Patton

Courage is almost a contradiction in terms. It
means a strong desire to live taking the form of
readiness to die.

G.K. Chesterton

True courage is not the brutal force of vulgar he-
roes, but the firm resolve of virture and reason.

Alfred North Whitehead

Courage is required not only in a person's occasional crucial decision for his own freedom, but in the little hour-to-hour decisions which place the bricks in the structure of his building of himself into a person who acts with freedom and responsibility.

Rollo May

It is curious—curious that physical courage should be so common in the world and moral courage so rare.

Mark Twain

Of those to whom much is given, much is required. And when at some future date the high court of history sits in judgment on each one of us—recording whether in our brief span of service we fulfilled our responsibilities to the state—our success or failure, in whatever office we may hold, will be measured by the answers to four questions: were we truly men of courage? . . . were we truly men of judgment? . . . were we truly men of integrity? . . . were we truly men of dedication?

John Fitzgerald Kennedy

Fear can keep a man out of danger, but courage can support him in it.

When we read, we fancy we could be martyrs; when we come to act, we cannot bear a provoking word.

Hannah More

Keep your fears to yourself, but share your courage with others.

Robert Louis Stevenson

A man of courage never wants weapons.

COURTESY

Too much courtesy is discourtesy.

Nothing is ever lost by courtesy. It is the cheapest
of pleasures, costs nothing, and conveys much. It
pleases him who gives and receives and thus,
like mercy, is twice blessed.

Erastus Wiman

COURTROOM

There is no greater indictment of judges
than the fact that honest men are afraid
to go into court, while criminals swagger
out its revolving doors.

Thomas Sowell

The penalty for laughing in a courtroom is six
months in jail; if it were not for this penalty, the
jury would never hear the evidence.

Henry Louis Mencken

COVET

The true way to gain much, is never to
desire to gain too much. He is not rich that
possesses much, but he that covets no more;
and he is not poor that enjoys little, but he
that wants too much.

Francis Beaumont

COWARD

Any coward can fight a battle when he's
sure of winning.

George Eliot

COWARDICE

Cowardice is not synonymous with prudence. It
often happens that the better part of
discretion is valor.

William Hazlitt

CREATIVITY

Creativity has been built into every one of us;
it's part of our design. Each of us lives less
of the life God intended for us when we choose
not to live out the creative
powers we possess.

Ted Engstrom

Creativity is the natural extension of
our enthusiasm.

Earl Nightingale

CREDIBILITY

Do what is expected of you . . . and you gain
credibility. Don't do what is expected of you . . .
and you lose credibility.

CREDIT

No man's credit is as good as his money.

Edgar Watson Howe

Credit Card: What you use to buy today what you can't afford tomorrow while you're still paying for it yesterday.

CRIME

The first anticrime bill was called the Ten Commandments.

Irv Kupcinet

The crime problem in New York is getting really serious. The other day the Statue of Liberty had both hands up.

Jay Leno

Small crimes always precede great ones. Never have we seen timid innocence pass suddenly to extreme licentiousness.

Jean Baptiste Racine

New York is an exciting town where something is happening all the time— most of it unsolved.

Johnny Carson

CRIMINALS

We don't give our criminals much punishment, but we sure give 'em plenty of publicity.

Will Rogers

CRISES

The wise man does not expose himself
needlessly to danger, since there are few things
for which he cares sufficiently; but he is willing, in
great crises, to give even his life—knowing that
under certain conditions it is not
worthwhile to live.

Aristotle

Every little thing counts in a crisis.

Jawaharlal Nehru

CRITICS

A critic is a gong at a railroad crossing
clanging loudly and vainly as the
train goes by.

Christopher Morley

Pay no attention to what the critics say; there
has never been set up a statue in
honor of a critic.

Jean Sibelius

Dear Mrs. Jones:
Thank you for your letter.
I shall try to do better.

Carl Sandburg

(form letter used for replying to critical letters)

CRITICISM

The trouble with most of us is that we would rather be ruined by praise than saved by criticism.

Dr. Norman Vincent Peale

Criticism may not be agreeable, but it is necessary. It fulfills the same function as pain in the human body: it calls attention to an unhealthy state of things.

Winston Churchill

People ask you for criticism, but they only want praise.

(William) Somerset Maugham

CRUELTY

All cruel people describe themselves as paragons of frankness.

Tennessee Williams

Cruelty, like every other vice, requires no motive outside of itself; it only requires opportunity.

George Eliot

CRUSADE

In the ancient recipe, the three antidotes for dullness or boredom are sleep, drink, and travel. It is rather feeble. From sleep you wake up, from drink you become sober, and from travel you come home again. And then where are you? No, the two sovereign remedies for dullness are love or a crusade.

D.H. Lawrence

CUNNING

The greatest cunning is to have none at all.

Carl Sandburg

CURIOSITY

Curiosity is one of the permanent and certain characteristics of a vigorous intellect.

Samuel Johnson

The important thing is not to stop questioning. Curiosity has its own reason for existing. One cannot help but be in awe when he contemplates the mysteries of eternity, of life, of the marvelous structure of reality. It is enough if one tries merely to comprehend a little of this mystery every day. Never lose a holy curiosity.

Albert Einstein

DANGER

One ought never to turn one's back on a
threatened danger and try to run away from it.
If you do that, you will double the danger.
But if you meet it promptly and without
flinching, you will reduce the danger by half.
Never run away from anything. Never!

Sir Winston Churchill

There is danger when a man throws
his tongue into high gear before he
gets his brain a-going.

C. C. Phelps

DARING

Far better it is to dare mighty things, to win
glorious triumphs, even though checkered by
failure, than to take rank with those poor spirits
who neither enjoy much nor suffer much,
because they live in the gray twilight that
knows neither victory nor defeat.

Theodore Roosevelt

No one reaches a high position
without daring.

Publilius Syrus

DARK SIDE

Everyone is a moon, and has a dark side which he never shows to anybody.

Mark Twain

DAUGHTER

My son is my son till he have got him a wife, but my daughter's my daughter all the days of her life.

Thomas Fuller

DAYS

Don't be fooled by the calendar. There are only as many days in the year as you make use of. One man gets only a week's value out of a year while another man gets a full year's value out of a week.

Charles Richards

DEARNESS

What we obtain too cheap, we esteem too lightly; 'tis dearness only that gives everything its value.

Thomas Paine

DEATH

He who would teach men to die, would teach them to live.

Montaigne

We need to be reminded that there is nothing morbid about honestly confronting the thought of life's end and preparing for it so that we may go gracefully and peacefully. The fact is, we cannot truly face life until we have learned to face the fact that it will be taken away from us.

Billy Graham

Do not seek death. Death will find you.
But seek the road which makes
death a fulfillment.

Dag Hammarskjold

Death comes when memories become more powerful to us than dreams.

One may live as a conqueror, a king, or a magistrate; but he must die a man. The bed of death brings every human being to his pure individuality, to the intense contemplation of that deepest and most solemn of all relations: the relation between the creature and his Creator.

Daniel Webster

Death is the golden key that opens the palace of eternity.

John Milton

Let death be daily before your eyes, and you will never entertain any abject thought, nor too eagerly covet anything.

Epictetus

We picture death as coming to destroy; let us rather picture Christ as coming to save. We think of death as ending; let us rather think of life as beginning, and that more abundantly. We think of losing; let us think of gaining. We think of parting, let us think of meeting. We think of going away; let us think of arriving. And as the voice of death whispers "You must go from earth," let us hear the voice of Christ saying, "You are but coming to Me!"

Norman Macleod

DEATH PENALTY

If we are to abolish the death penalty, I should like to see the first step taken by my friends the murderers.

Alphonse Karr

DEBT

Debt is the worst poverty.

Thomas Fuller

Some people use one half their ingenuity to get into debt, and the other half to avoid paying it.

George D. Prentice

DECEPTION

All deception in the course of life is indeed nothing else but a lie reduced to practice, and falsehood passing from words into things.

Robert South

DECISIVENESS

It does not take much strength to do things, but it
requires great strength to decide
on what to do.

Elbert Hubbard

Whenever you see a successful business,
someone once made a courageous decision.

Peter Drucker

The moment one definitely commits oneself, then
Providence moves too. All sorts of things occur to
help that would never otherwise have occured. A
stream of events issues from the decision, raising
unforeseen incidents and meetings and material
assistance, which no man could have
dreamt would have come his way.

W.H. Murray

Whenever I make a bum decision, I go out
and make another one.

Harry Truman

Deliberate with caution, but act with
decision and promptness.

Charles Caleb Colton

Be willing to make decisions. That's the most
important quality of a good leader. Don't fall victim
to what I call the ready-aim-aim-aim syndrome.
You must be willing to fire.

T. Boone Pickens

In forty hours I shall be in battle, with little
information, and on the spur of the moment
will have to make the most momentous
decisions. But I believe that one's spirit
enlarges with responsibility and that, with
God's help, I shall make them, and
make them right.

General George S. Patton

My father was my idol. I tried to emulate
him not only as an ideal soldier but as
a great man. He used to say: "Gather all the facts
possible and then make your decision on what
you think is right, as opposed to what you think is
wrong. Don't try to guess what others will think,
whether they will praise or deride you. And
always remember that at least some of your
decisions will probably be wrong. Do this and
you always will sleep well at night."

Douglas MacArthur

DEDICATION

Give me 100 men who fear nothing but sin and
desire nothing but God, and I care not whether
they be clergy or laymen; such men alone will
shake the gates of hell and set up the Kingdom
of Heaven on earth.

John Wesley

DEEDS

Thunder without rain is like words
without deeds.

Those who aim at great deeds must
also suffer greatly.

Plutarch

People may doubt what you say but they
will believe what you do.

Do what you can, with what you have,
where you are.

Theodore Roosevelt

Some people dream of worthy accomplishments,
while others stay awake and do them.

As I grow older I pay less attention to what men
say. I just watch what they do.

Andrew Carnegie

The only measure of what you believe is what
you do. If you want to know what people believe,
don't read what they write, don't ask them what
they believe, just observe what they do.

Ashley Montague

To know what has to be done, then
do it, comprises the whole philosophy
of practical life.

Sir William Osler

A man of words and not of deeds is
like a garden full of weeds.

He does not believe that does not live
according to his belief.

Thomas Fuller

They do not love that do not show their love.

William Shakespeare

By his deeds we know a man.

Men are alike in their promises. It is only in their
deeds that they differ.

Molière

What one does, one becomes.

DEFEAT

It is defeat that turns bone to flint, and gristle to
muscle, and makes men invincible, and forms
those heroic natures that are now in ascendency
in the world. Do not then be afraid of defeat. You
are never so near to victory as when defeated
in a good cause.

Henry Ward Beecher

What is defeat? Nothing but education; nothing
but the first step to something better.

Wendell Phillips

Those who are prepared to die for any cause
are seldom defeated.

Jawaharlal Nehru

DEFECTS

Scoff not at the natural defects of any which are not in their power to amend. It is cruel to beat a cripple with his own crutches!

Thomas Fuller

DEFENSE

One sword keeps another in the sheath.

George Herbert

DEFINITION

A large part of the discussions of disputants comes from the want of accurate definition. Let one define his terms and then stick to the definition, and half the differences in philosophy and theology would come to an end, and be seen to have no real foundation.

Tryon Edwards

DELUSION

All are lunatics, but he who can analyze his delusion is called a philosopher.

Ambrose Bierce

DEMOCRACY

Democracy is based upon the conviction that there are extraordinary possibilities in ordinary people.

Harry Emerson Fosdick

Too many people expect wonders from democracy, when the most wonderful thing of all is just having it.

Walter Winchell

In a democracy, the individual enjoys not only the ultimate power but carries the ultimate responsibility.

Norman Cousins

Man's capacity for justice makes democracy possible; but man's inclination to injustice makes deomocracy necessary.

Reinhold Niebuhr

Human dignity, economic freedom, individual responsibility, these are the characteristics that distinguish democracy from all other forms devised by man.

Dwight David Eisenhower

Democracy, the practice of self-government, is a covenant among free men to respect the rights and liberties of their fellows.

Franklin Delano Roosevelt

The measure of a democracy is the measure of the freedom of its humblest citizens.

John Galsworthy

DEMOCRATS

Democrats can't get elected unless things get worse, and things won't get worse unless they get elected.

Jeane Kirkpatrick

DENIED

Never believe anything until it has been officially denied.

Claud Cockburn

DEPARTURE

There is a time for departure even when there's no certain place to go.

Tennessee Williams

DEPRESSION

Depression comes, not from having faults, but from the refusal to face them. There are tens of thousands of persons today suffering from fears which in reality are nothing but the effects of hidden sins.

Fulton John Sheen

DESIRE

If you don't get everything you want, think of the things you don't get that you don't want.

Oscar Wilde

We soon believe what we desire.

Nobody speaks the truth when there's something they must have.

Elizabeth Bowen

If you desire many things, many things will seem but a few.

Benjamin Franklin

If your desires be endless, your cares
and fears will be so too.

Thomas Fuller

I count him braver who overcomes his
desires than him who conquers his enemies;
the hardest victory is the victory over self.

Aristotle

DESPAIR

Hope deferred maketh the heart sick.

Proverbs 13:12

DESPISE

He who despises himself esteems
himself as a self-despiser.

Susan Sontag

DESPONDENCY

How many feasible projects have miscarried
through despondency, and been strangled in their
birth by a cowardly imagination?

Jeremy Collier

DETERMINATION

This one thing I do . . . I press on toward
the mark. . . .

Philippians 3:13,14

It takes as much courage to have tried and failed
as it does to have tried and succeeded.

Anne Morrow Lindbergh

One can go a long way after one is tired.

No matter what business you're in, you can't run in place or someone will pass you by. It doesn't matter how many games you've won.

Jim Valvano

Be like a postage stamp—stick to one thing until you get there.

Josh Billings

You can't try to do things; you simply must do them.

Ray Bradbury

An ant hole may collapse an embankment.

The heights by great men reached and kept
Were not attained by sudden flight,
But they, while their companions slept
Were toiling upward in the night.

Henry Wadsworth Longfellow

Hold on with a bulldog grip, and chew and choke as much as possible.

Abraham Lincoln

Some men give up their designs when they have almost reached the goal; while others, on the contrary, obtain a victory by exerting, at the last moment, more vigorous efforts than before.

Polybius

The real difference between men is energy. A strong will, a settled purpose, an invincible determination, can accomplish almost anything; and in this lies the distinction between great men and little men.

Thomas Fuller

Firmness of purpose is one of the most necessary sinews of character, and one of the best instruments of success. Without it genius wastes its efforts in a maze of inconsistencies.

Philip Dormer Stanhope

We fight to great disadvantage when we fight with those who have nothing to lose.

Francesco Guicciardini

DIFFICULT

Undertake something that is difficult; it will do you good. Unless you try to do something beyond what you have already mastered, you will never grow.

Ronald E. Osborn

Nothing is particularly hard if you divide it into small jobs.

Henry Ford

DIFFICULTIES

There are two ways of meeting difficulties: you alter the difficulties or you alter yourself meeting them.

Phyllis Bottome

The beauty of the soul shines out when
a man bears with composure one
heavy mischance after another,
not because he does not feel them,
but because he is a man of high
and heroic temper.

Aristotle

Difficulties strengthen the mind, as
labor does the body.

Seneca

Difficulties are God's errands; and when we
are sent upon them we should esteem it a
proof of God's confidence—as a
compliment from him.

Henry Ward Beecher

The habits of a vigorous mind are formed
in contending with difficulties . . . great
necessities call out great virtues.

Abigail Adams

I am grateful for all my problems. After each
one was overcome, I became stronger and
more able to meet those that were still to come.
I grew in all my difficulties.

J. C. Penney

Every difficulty slurred over will be a ghost
to disturb your repose later on.

Frederic Chopin

The greater the difficulty the more glory
in surmounting it.

Epicurus

DIGNITY

Originality and the feeling of one's own
dignity are achieved only through work
and struggle.

Fyodor Dostoyevsky

DILIGENCE

What we hope ever to do with ease, we must
learn first to do with diligence.

Samuel Johnson

Few things are impossible to diligence and
skill . . . Great works are performed, not by
strength, but perseverance.

Samuel Johnson

It is easier to get people to promise to do
better tomorrow than it is to get them to
do their best today.

So teach us to number our days, that we may
apply our hearts unto wisdom.

Psalm 90:12

Always do more than is required of you

For the diligent, the week has seven todays,
for the slothful seven tomorrows.

DIRTY DISHES

Thank God for dirty dishes; they
have a tale to tell.
While other folks go hungry, we're
eating pretty well.
With home, and health, and happiness,
we shouldn't want to fuss;
For by this stack of evidence,
God's very good to us.

DISAGREEMENT

The people to fear are not those who disagree
with you, but those who disagree with you and
are too cowardly to let you know.

Napoleon Bonaparte

DISCERNMENT

After a spirit of discernment, the next rarest
things in the world are diamonds and pearls.

Jean de la Bruyere

DISCIPLINE

Better the child should cry than the father.

The secret of discipline is motivation. When
a man is sufficiently motivated, discipline
will take care of itself.

Sir Alexander Paterson

You never will be the person you can be
if pressure, tension, and discipline are
taken out of your life.

James G. Bilkey

Make it a point to do something every day that
you don't want to do. This is the golden rule for
acquiring the habit of doing your
duty without pain.

Mark Twain

DISCONTENT

Discontent is the first step in progress.

DISCORD

Tranquility will roof a house, but discord can
wear away the foundations of a city.

Ernest Bramah

DISCOVERIES

Great discoveries and improvements invariably
involve the cooperation of many minds. I may be
given credit for having blazed the trail but when I
look at the subsequent developments I feel the
credit is due to others rather than to myself.

Alexander Graham Bell

DISCRETION

Nothing more dangerous than a friend without
discretion; even a prudent enemy is preferable.

Jean de la Fontaine

Better a lean agreement than a fat lawsuit.

DISCUSSION

I don't like to talk much with people who always agree with me. It is amusing to coquette with an echo for a little while, but one soon tires of it.

Thomas Carlyle

DISHONESTY

Dishonesty, cowardice, and duplicity are never impulsive.

George A. Knight

DISORDER

When the 1968 Democratic convention was held in Chicago, then-Mayor Richard Daley said at a press conference, "The police are here not to create disorder. They are here to preserve disorder."

DISORGANIZATION

He that is everywhere is nowhere.

Thomas Fuller

DISPOSITION

It isn't our position, but our disposition, that makes us happy.

The Constitution of America only guarantees
pursuit of happiness—you have to catch up with it
yourself. Fortunately, happiness is something that
depends not on position but on disposition, and
life is what you make it.

Gill Robb Wilson

DISPUTE

If two friends ask you to judge a dispute, don't
accept, because you will lose one friend; on the
other hand, if two strangers come with the same
request, accept because you will gain one friend.

Saint Augustine

In private life I never knew anyone interfere
with other people's disputes but that he
heartily repented of it.

Thomas Carlyle

DISSENT

Dissent does not include the freedom to
destroy the system of law which guarantees
freedom to speak, assemble, and march in
protest. Dissent is not anarchy.

Seymour F. Simon

DISSOLUTION

Let dissolution come when it will, it can do
the Christian no harm, for it will be but a
passage out of a prison into a palace; out of a
sea of troubles into a haven of rest; out of a
crowd of enemies to an innumerable company of
true, loving, and faithful friends; out of shame,
reproach, and contempt into
exceeding great and eternal glory.

John Bunyan

DISTRUST

What loneliness is more lonely than distrust?

George Eliot

DIVERSITY

One man's meat is another man's poison.

DIVORCE

Weddings are always the same, but
no divorces are alike.

Will Rogers

What a holler would ensue if people
had to pay the minister as much to marry them as
they have to pay a lawyer to get them a divorce.

Claire Trevor

DOCTOR

Your three best doctors are faith,
time, and patience.

DOG

Outside of a dog, a book is man's best friend.
Inside of a dog, it's too dark to read.

Groucho Marx

The dog was created specially for children.

Henry Ward Beecher

DOGMA

You can't teach an old dogma new tricks.

Dorothy Parker

DOING

The Christian life is not merely knowing or
hearing, but doing the will of Christ.

Frederick William Robertson

I feel that the greatest reward for doing is the
opportunity to do more.

Jonas Edward Salk

DOWN

He that is down needs fear no fall.

John Bunyan

DRAMA

Drama is life with the dull bits cut out.

Alfred Hitchcock

DREAMS

It takes a lot of courage to show your dreams to someone else.

Erma Bombeck

The future belongs to those who believe in the beauty of their dreams.

Eleanor Roosevelt

If a man wants his dreams to come true, he must wake up.

Dreams have only one owner at a time. That's why dreamers are lonely.

Erma Bombeck

All our dreams can come true—if we have the courage to pursue them.

Walt Disney

DRIVE

If your wife wants to learn to drive, don't stand in her way.

Sam Levenson

DRUNKENNESS

The sight of a drunkard is a better sermon against that vice than the best that was ever preached on the subject.

John Faucit Saville

Drunkenness is simply voluntary insanity.

Seneca

Drunkenness is not a mere matter of
intoxicating liquors; it goes deeper—far
deeper. Drunkenness is the failure of a man to
control his thoughts.

David Grayson

DRAMA

A talent for drama is not a talent for
writing, but is an ability to articulate
human relationships.

Gore Vidal

DUDE

What kind of car does a dude drive?
A Dude-a-baker.

Nick Arnette

DUTY

My observation is that whenever one person is
found adequate to the discharge of duty by close
application thereto, it is worse executed by two
persons, and scarcely done at all if three or
more are employed therein.

George Washington

Duty: Something one looks forward to without
pleasure, does with reluctance, and boasts
about afterwards.

Let us have faith that right makes might, and
in that faith, let us to the end dare to do our duty
as we understand it.

Abraham Lincoln

The consideration that human happiness and moral duty are inseparably connected, will always continue to prompt me to promote the former by inculcating the practice of the latter.

George Washington

Do the duty which lies nearest thee. Thy second duty will already have become clearer.

Thomas Carlyle

Do not plan for ventures before finishing what's at hand.

Euripides

Happiness is the natural flower of duty.

Phillips Brooks

An unwillingness to do little things often gets people into big trouble.

Seek happiness for its own sake, and you will not find it; seek for duty, and happiness will follow, as the shadow comes with the sunshine.

Tryon Edwards

The habit of doing one's duty drives away fear.

Charles Baudelaire

Never mind your happiness; do your duty.

Will Durant

The path of duty lies in the thing that is nearby,
but men seek it in things far off.

Everyone must row with the oars he has.

I firmly believe that any man's finest hour—his
greatest fulfillment to all he holds dear—is that
moment when he has worked his heart out
in a good cause and lies exhausted on the
field of battle victorious.

Vince Lombardi

Without duty, life is soft and boneless.

Joseph Joubert

All men are afraid in battle. The coward is the one
who lets his fear overcome his sense of duty.
Duty is the essence of manhood.

General George S. Patton

DYING

Someone should tell us right at the start
that we are dying. Then we would be more
inclined to live life to the limit every
minute of every day.

Michael Landon

EARLY RISING

It is well to be up before daybreak,
for such habits contribute to health,
wealth, and wisdom.

Aristotle

EATING

Part of the secret of success in life is
to eat what you like and let the food
fight it out inside.

Mark Twain

I saw few die of hunger; of eating,
a hundred thousand.

Benjamin Franklin

EATING CROW

"Eating crow" is never pleasant—no matter how
much mustard and ketchup you put on it. But
usually the sooner you eat it the less
unpleasant it is to the taste!

Nido Qubein

ECONOMIST

In all recorded history there has not been one economist who has had to worry about where the next meal would come from.

Peter F. Drucker

EDUCATION

I have never let my schooling interfere with my education.

Mark Twain

You cannot teach a child to take care of himself unless you will let him try to take care of himself. He will make mistakes; and out of these mistakes will come his wisdom.

Henry Ward Beecher

The best education in the world is that by struggling to get a living.

Wendel Phillips

EFFICIENCY

It is more than probable that the average man could, with no injury to his health, increase his efficiency fifty percent.

Sir Walter Scott

EFFORT

It is hard to fail, but it is worse never to have tried to succeed. In this life we get nothing save by effort.

Theodore Roosevelt

Effort only fully releases its reward after a person refuses to quit.

Napoleon Hill

ELOQUENCE

True eloquence consists of saying all that should be said, and that only.

François de la Rochefoucauld

EMPLOYMENT

When you hire people that are smarter than you are, you prove you are smarter than they are.

R. H. Grant

ENABLEMENT

What God expects us to attempt, He also enables us to achieve.

Stephen Olford

ENCOURAGEMENT

Appreciation is thanking, recognition is seeing, and encouragement is bringing hope for the future.

ENDURANCE

To endure is the first thing that a child ought
to learn, and that which he will have
the most need to know.

Jean Jacques Rousseau

To struggle when hope is banished.
To live when life's salt is gone!
To dwell in a dream that's vanished
To endure, and go calmly on!

Ben Johnson

ENEMIES

Am I not destroying my enemies
when I make friends of them?

Abraham Lincoln

Forgive your enemies, but never
forget their names.

John F. Kennedy

Everyone needs a warm personal enemy
or two to keep him free of rust in the
movable parts of his mind.

Gene Fowler

Better a thousand enemies outside the
house than one inside.

Men of sense often learn from their enemies. Prudence is the best safeguard. This principal cannot be learned from a friend, but an enemy extorts it immediately. It is from their foes, not their friends, that cities learn the lesson of building high walls and ships of war. And this lesson saves their children, their homes, and their properties.

Aristophanes

If you knew how cowardly your enemy is, you would slap him.

Egar Watson Howe

In order to have an enemy, one must be somebody. One must be a force before he can be resisted by another force. A malicious enemy is better than a clumsy friend.

Anne Sophie Swetchine

ENFORCE

What you cannot enforce, do not command.

Sophocles

ENTHUSIASM

The world is moved by highly motivated people, by enthusiasts, by men and women who want something very much or believe very much.

John Gardner

We act as though comfort and luxury were the chief requirements of life, when all that we need to make us happy is something to be enthusiastic about.

Charles Kingsley

I prefer the errors of enthusiasm to the indifference of wisdom.

Anatole France

No one keeps up his enthusiasm automatically. Enthusiasm must be nourished with new actions, new aspirations, new efforts, new vision. Compete with yourself; set your teeth and dive into the job of breaking your own record.

When we accept tough jobs as a challenge and wade into them with joy and enthusiasm, miracles can happen.

Arland Gilbert

No person who is enthusiastic about his work has anything to fear from life.

Samuel Goldwyn

ENVY

Love looks through a telescope; envy, through a microscope.

Henry Wheeler Shaw

The envious man does not die only once but as many times as the person he envies lives to hear the voice of praise.

Baltasar Gracian

Envy always implies conscious inferiority
wherever it resides.

Pliny the Elder

The envious praise only that which they can
surpass; that which surpasses
them they censure.

Charles Caleb Colton

Men of noble birth are noted to be envious
toward new men when they rise, for the distance
is altered; it is like a deceit of the eye, that when
others come on they think themselves go back.

Francis Bacon

Envy's memory is nothing but a row of hooks to
hang up grudges on.

John Watson Foster

Envy eats nothing but its own heart.

Envy is more irreconcilable than hatred.

François de la Rochefoucauld

Nothing sharpens sight like envy.

Thomas Fuller

As iron is eaten away by rust, so the envious are
consumed by their own passion.

Antisthenes

EPIGRAM

An epigram is a half-truth so stated as to irritate
the person who believes the other half.

Shailer Mathews

EQUAL

We believe, as asserted in the Declaration of
Independence, that all men are created equal;
but that does not mean that all men are
or can be equal in possessions, in ability,
or in merit; it simply means that all shall
stand equal before the law.

William Jennings Bryan

We hold these truths to be self-evident that all
men are created equal, that they are endowed by
their Creator with certain unalienable Rights, that
among these are Life, Liberty, and the
pursuit of Happiness.

Thomas Jefferson

EQUALITY

Americans are so enamored of equality that
they would rather be equal in slavery
than unequal in freedom.

Alexis de Tocqueville

ERROR

It takes less time to do a thing right than it
does to explain why you did it wrong.

Henry Wadsworth Longfellow

EVALUATION

People travel to wonder at the height of mountains, at the huge waves of the sea, at the long courses of rivers, at the vast compass of the ocean, at the circular motion of the stars, and they pass by themselves without wondering.

Saint Augustine

Man's most valuable trait is a judicious sense of what not to believe.

Euripides

EVERLASTING LIFE

For God so loved the world, that he gave his only begotten Son, that whosoever believeth in him should not perish, but have everlasting life.

John 3:16

EVIL

Evil events come from evil causes; and what we suffer springs, generally, from what we have done.

Aristophanes

He who passively accepts evil is as much involved in it as he who helps to perpetrate it.

Martin Luther King, Jr.

It is the law of our humanity that man must know good through evil. No great principle ever triumphed but through much evil. No man ever progressed to greatness and goodness but through great mistakes.

Frederick W. Robertson

I never wonder to see men wicked, but I often wonder to see them not ashamed.

Jonathan Swift

He who is strong in evil deeds is also strong in good.

The wicked flee when no man pursueth, but they make better time when someone is after them.

Charles Henry Parkhurst

EXAGGERATION

There are people so addicted to exaggeration they can't tell the truth without lying.

Josh Billings

EXAMPLE

I have learned silence from the talkative, toleration from the intolerant, and kindness from the unkind; yet strange, I am ungrateful to these teachers.

Kahlil Gibran

First find the man in yourself if you will inspire manliness in others.

Amos Bronson Alcott

EXCELLENCE

The quality of a person's life is in direct proportion
to their commitment to excellence, regardless of
their chosen field of endeavor.

Vince Lombardi

EXCEPTION

I know of no manner of speaking so offensive
as that of giving praise, and closing it with
an exception.

Sir Richard Steele

EXCITEMENT

Human nature, if it healthy, demands
excitement; and if it does not obtain its
thrilling excitement in the right way,
it will seek it in the wrong. God never
makes bloodless stoics; He makes
no passionless saints.

Oswald Chambers

EXCUSE

An excuse is worse and more terrible than
a lie; for an excuse is a lie guarded.

Alexander Pope

EXECUTIVE

The best executive is the one who has sense enough to pick good men to do what he wants done, and the self-restraint to keep from meddling with them while they do it.

Theodore Roosevelt

EXPECTATION

We part more easily with what we possess than with our expectations of what we hope for: expectation always goes beyond enjoyment.

Henry Home

The best part of our lives we pass in counting on what is to come.

William Hazlitt

Men . . . always think that something they are going to get is better than what they have got.

John Oliver Hobbes

Too many people miss the silver lining because they're expecting gold.

Maurice Setter

EXPERIENCE

Experience is something you get too late to do anything about the mistakes you made while getting it.

Men are wise in proportion, not to their experience, but to their capacity for experience.

George Bernard Shaw

Experience is not what happens to you;
it is what you do with what
happens to you.

Aldous Huxley

Education is what a fellow gets from
reading the fine print. Experience is what
he gets if he doesn't read it.

EYE

An eye can threaten like a loaded and leveled
gun, or it can insult like hissing or kicking; or,
in its altered mood, by beams of kindness,
it can make the heart dance for joy.

Ralph Waldo Emerson

FABLES

Fables, like parables, are more ancient
than formal arguments and are often the
most effective means of presenting and
impressing both truth and duty.

Tryon Edwards

FACE IT

Facing it—always facing it—that's the way
to get through. Face it!

Joseph Conrad

FACT

If a man will kick a fact out of the window,
when he comes back he finds it again
in the chimney corner.

Ralph Waldo Emerson

There is no sadder sight in the world than
to see a beautiful theory killed
by a brutal fact.

Thomas Henry Huxley

Once the facts are clear, the decisions
jump out at you.

Peter Drucker

FAILURE

Failure is the opportunity to begin again
more intelligently.

Henry Ford

The person who succeeds is not the one who
holds back, fearing failure, nor the one who
never fails . . . but rather the one who
moves on in spite of failure.

Charles Swindoll

Many of life's failures are people who did
not realize how close they were to success
when they gave up.

Thomas Edison

He who has never failed somewhere, that
man cannot be great.

Herman Melville

Failure is usually the line of least persistence.

Wilfred Beaver

Never give a man up until he has failed
at something he likes.

Lewis E. Lawes

FAITH

Faith is a gift of God.

Blaise Pascal

Faith is the divine evidence whereby the spiritual man discerneth God, and the things of God.

John Wesley

Faith is like radar that sees through the fog the reality of things at a distance that the human eye cannot see.

Corrie ten Boom

Pity the human being who is not able to connect faith within himself with the infinite. . . . He who has faith has . . . an inward reservoir of courage, hope, confidence, calmness, and assuring trust that all will come out well—even though to the world it may appear to come out most badly.

B.C. Forbes

This is the art of courage: to see things as they are and still believe that the victory lies not with those who avoid the bad, but those who taste, in living awareness, every drop of the good.

Victoria Lincoln

Faith makes the uplook good, the outlook bright, the inlook favorable, and the future glorious.

V. Raymond Edman

I have fought a good fight, I have finished my course, I have kept the faith.

2 Timothy 4:7

Faith is putting all your eggs in God's basket, then counting your blessings before they hatch.

Ramona C. Carroll

The just shall live by faith.

Romans 1:17

Scepticism has never founded empires, established principles, or changed the world's heart. The great doers in history have always been men of faith.

Edwin Hubbel Chapin

Any featherhead can have confidence in times of victory, but the test is to have faith when things are going wrong.

Winston Churchill

Faith is a Fantastic Adventure In Trusting Him.

Corrie ten Boom

God hasn't called me to be successful. He's called me to be faithful.

Mother Teresa

FAITHFULNESS

Nothing is more noble, nothing more venerable than fidelity. Faithfulness and truth are the most sacred excellences and endowments of the human mind.

Cicero

FALSEHOOD

The telling of a falsehood is like the cut of a sabre; for though the wound may heal, the scar of it will remain.

Saadi (Muslih-ud-Din)

Falsehood often lurks upon the tongue of him
who, by self-praise, seeks to enhance his
value in the eyes of others.

James Gordon Bennett

Falsehoods not only disagree with truths,
but they usually quarrel
among themselves.

Daniel Webster

FALSE REPORT

One false report sets ten thousand
people to believe it.

FAME

The lust of fame is the last that a
wise man shakes off.

Tacitus

Fame usually comes to those who
are thinking about something else.

Horace Greeley

Let us satisfy our own consciences, and trouble
not ourselves by looking for fame. If we deserve
it, we shall attain it: if we deserve it not, we
cannot force it. The praise bad actions obtain dies
soon away; if good deeds are at first
unworthily received, they are afterward
more properly appreciated.

Seneca

FAMILIARITY

Familiarity is a magician that is cruel to
beauty but kind to ugliness.

Ouida

Though familiarity may not breed contempt,
it takes off the edge of admiration.

William Hazlitt

FAMILY

Happy families are alike; every unhappy
family is unhappy in its own way.

Leo Tolstoy

At the end only two things really matter to a
man, regardless of who he is, and they are the
affection and understanding of his family.
Anything and everything else he creates is
insubstantial; it is a ship given over to the mercy
of the winds and tides of prejudice. But the family
is an everlasting anchorage, a quiet harbor where
a man's ship can be left to swing to the
moorings of pride and loyalty.

Richard E. Byrd

Where can a man better be than with his family?

Jean Francois Marmontel

FASHION

As to matters of dress, I would recommend one
never to be first in the fashion nor the last out of it.

John Wesley

The custom and fashion of today will be the awkwardness and outrage of tomorrow—so arbitrary are these transient laws.

Alexandre Dumas

FATHER

The most important thing a father can do for his children is to love their mother.

Theodore Martin Hesburgh

By profession I am a soldier and take pride in that fact. But I am prouder—infinitely prouder—to be a father. A soldier destroys in order to build; the father only builds, never destroys. The one has the potentiality of death; the other embodies creation and life. And while the hordes of death are mighty, the battalions of life are mightier still. It is my hope that my son, when I am gone, will remember me not from the battle but in the home repeating with him our simple daily prayer.

Douglas MacArthur

FATIGUE

Nothing is so fatiguing as the eternal hanging on of an uncompleted task.

William James

Fatigue makes cowards of us all.

Vince Lombardi

FAULTS

We confess to little faults, only to persuade
ourselves that we have no great ones.

François de la Rochefoucauld

The fault, dear Brutus, is not in our stars,
but in ourselves.

William Shakespeare

To reprove small faults with undue vehemence
is as absurd as if a man should take a great
hammer to kill a fly on his friend's forehead.

Think of your faults the first part of the night when
you are awake, and the faults of others the latter
part of the night when you are asleep.

The camel never sees its own hump, but that of
its brother is always before its eye.

Faults are thick where love is thin.

FAVOR

To accept a favor from a friend is to confer one.

John Churton Collins

FEAR

The most drastic and usually the most
effective remedy for fear is direct action.

William Burnham

It is only the fear of God that can deliver
us from the fear of man.

John Witherspoon

We must face what we fear; that is the case of
the core of the restoration of health.

Max Lerner

The fear of the LORD is the beginning of wisdom.

Psalm 111:10

If you wish to fear nothing, consider that
everything is to be feared.

Marcus Annaeus Seneca

Fear is the dark room in which negatives
are developed.

The man who fears suffering is already
suffering from what he fears.

Michel de Montaigne

I sought the LORD, and He heard me, and
delivered me from all my fears.

Psalm 34:4

Many of our fears are tissuepaper-thin, and
a single courageous step would carry us
clear through them.

Brendan Francis

FIGHT

When two elephants fight, it is the grass
underneath that suffers.

FINANCE

Alexander Hamilton originated the put-and-take
system in our national treasury: the taxpayers
put it in and the politicians take it out.

Will Rogers

FIRE

Better a little fire to warm us than a great
one to burn us.

Thomas Fuller

FLAB

Muscles come and go; flab lasts.

Bill Vaughan

FLATTERY

All are not friends that speak us fair.

We sometimes think we hate flattery, when we
only hate the manner in which we have
been flattered.

François de la Rochefoucauld

Some there are who profess to despise all flattery,
but even these are, nevertheless, to be flattered,
by being told that they do despise it.

Charles Caleb Colton

Flattery is never so agreeable as to our blind side; commend a fool for his wit, or a knave for his honesty, and they will receive you into their bosom.

Henry Fielding

He who praises everybody, praises nobody.

Samuel Johnson

FOCUS

What we love to do we find time to do.

John Lancaster Spalding

The shortest way to do many things is to do only one thing at a time.

Richard Cecil

When a man knows he is to be hanged in a fortnight, it concentrates his mind wonderfully.

Samuel Johnson

FOOL

If I want to look at a fool, I have only to look in the mirror.

Seneca

I wasn't born a fool. It took work to get this way.

Danny Kaye

Answer a fool according to his folly, lest he be wise in his own conceit.

Proverbs 26:5

A fool may be known by six things: anger, without cause; speech, without profit; change, without progress; inquiry, without object; putting trust in a stranger; and mistaking foes for friends.

Fools rush in—and get all the best seats.

Marybeth Weston

Fools! not to know how health and temperance bless the rustic swain, while luxury destroys her pampered train.

Hesiod

FOOLISHNESS

There is a foolish corner in the brain of the wisest man.

Aristotle

FORBIDDEN

Adam was but human—this explains it all. He did not want the apple for the apple's sake, he wanted it only because it was forbidden. The mistake was not forbidding the serpent; then he would have eaten the serpent.

Mark Twain

FORCE

Force is all-conquering, but its victories are short-lived.

Abraham Lincoln

FORGIVE

I firmly believe a great many prayers are not answered because we are not willing to forgive someone.

Dwight L. Moody

If the other person injures you, you may forget the injury; but if you injure him you will always remember.

Kahlil Gibran

When you forgive your enemies, you weaken them.

It is easier to forgive an enemy than a friend.

Madame Dorothee Deluzy

One of the secrets of a long and fruitful life is to forgive everybody everything every night before you go to bed.

If thou wouldst find much favor and peace with God and man, be very low in thine own eyes. Forgive thyself little and others much.

Robert Leighton

FORGIVENESS

Let all bitterness, and wrath, and anger, and clamour, and evil speaking, be put away from you, with all malice: and be ye kind one to another, tenderhearted, forgiving one another, even as God for Christ's sake hath forgiven you.

Ephesians 4:31,32

Forgiveness is the oil of relationships.

Josh McDowell

The fragrance of the violet sheds on the heel
that has crushed it.

Mark Twain

Forgiveness means letting go of the past.

Gerald Jampolsky

Forgiveness is not an elective in the curriculum of
life. It is a required course, and the exams are
always tough to pass.

Charles Swindoll

The remedy for wrongs is to forget them.

Publilius Syrus

The more a man knows the more he forgives.

Catherine the Great

Forgiveness needs to be accepted, as well as
offered, before it is complete.

C.S. Lewis

A Christian will find it cheaper to pardon than to
resent. Forgiveness saves the expense of anger,
the cost of hatred, the waste of spirits.

Hannah More

If men wound you with injuries, meet them with
patience: hasty words rankle the wound, soft
language dresses it, forgiveness cures it, and
oblivion takes away the scar. It is more noble by
silence to avoid an injury than by argument
to overcome it.

Francis Beaumont

FREE

No man is free who is not a master of himself.

Epictetus

FREEDOM

The greatest glory of a free-born people is to transmit that freedom to their children.

William Havard

We have confused the free with the free and easy.

Adlai Stevenson

If a man does only what is required of him, he is a slave. The moment he does more, he is a free man.

A.W. Robertson

Society is continually pushing in on the individual. He has only a few areas in which he can be himself, free from external restraint or observation.

Edward Vaughan Long

Freedom is not procured by a full enjoyment of what is desired, but by controlling that desire.

Epictetus

We can be thankful to a friend for a few acres, or a little money; and yet for the freedom and command of the whole earth, and for the great benefits of our being, our life, health, and reason, we look upon ourselves as under no obligation.

Seneca

FRESH AIR

I remember when people used to step
outside a moment for a breath of fresh air. Now
sometimes you have to step outside for days
before you get it.

Victor Borge

FRIEND

Give me the avowed, the erect, the manly foe,
bold I can meet, perhaps may turn his blow! But
of all plagues, good Heavens, thy wrath can send,
save, save, oh save me from the candid friend!

George Canning

Every man, however wise, needs the advice of
some sagacious friend in the affairs of life.

Plautus

He's a fine friend. He stabs you in the front.

Leonard Louis Levinson

The happiest miser on earth is the man who
saves up every friend he can make.

Robert E. Sherwood

Be slow in choosing a friend, slower in changing.

Benjamin Franklin

A friend is someone you can do nothing with,
and enjoy it.

One loyal friend is worth ten thousand relatives.

Euripides

The friend of my adversity I shall always cherish most. I can better trust those who helped to relieve the gloom of my dark hours than those who are so ready to enjoy with me the sunshine of my prosperity.

Ulysses S. Grant

If we all told what we know of one another, there would not be four friends in the world.

Blaise Pascal

When the character of someone is not clear to you, look at that person's friends.

We shall never have friends if we expect to find them without fault.

Thomas Fuller

Be careful the environment you choose, for it will shape you; be careful the friends you choose, for you will become like them.

W. Clement Stone

Cheerful company shortens the miles.

The best way to keep your friends is not to give them away.

Wilson Mizner

Friends agree best at a distance.

There are three kinds of friends: best friends, guest friends, and pest friends.

Laurence J. Peter

Two persons cannot long be friends if they cannot forgive each other's little failings.

Jean de la Bruyere

You can make more friends in two months by becoming interested in other people than you can in two years by trying to get other people interested in you.

Dale Carnegie

FRIENDLY

Lead the life that will make you kindly and friendly to everyone about you, and you will be surprised what a happy life you will live.

Charles M. Schwab

FRIENDSHIP

Friendship is the inexpressible comfort of feeling safe with a person, having neither to weigh thoughts nor measure words.

George Eliot

Friendship doesn't make you wealthy, but true friendship will reveal the wealth within you. True friendship comes when silence between two people is comfortable.

Dave Tyson Gentry

Don't flatter yourself that friendship authorizes you to say disagreeable things to your intimates. The nearer you come into relation with a person, the more necessary do tact and courtesy become.

Oliver Wendell Holmes

FUN

There is no fun in having nothing to do; the fun is having lots to do and not doing it.

Francis Herbert Bradley

FUTURE

The strongest are those who renounce their own times and become a living part of those yet to come. The strongest, and the rarest.

Milovan Djilas

Your future depends on many things, but mostly on you.

Frank Tyger

The best thing about the future is that it comes only one day at a time.

Abraham Lincoln

The future has several names. For the weak, it is the impossible. For the fainthearted, it is the unknown. For the thoughtful and valiant, it is ideal.

Victor Hugo

The future is like heaven—everyone exalts it but no one wants to go there now.

James Baldwin

The future belongs to people who see possibilities before they become obvious.

Ted Levitt

When all else is lost, the future still remains.

Christian Nestell Bovee

GAIN

Mankind never loses any good things, physical,
intellectual, or moral, till it finds a better, and
then the loss is a gain. No steps backward, is
the rule of human history. What is gained by one
man is invested in all men, and is a permanent
investment for all time.

Theodore Parker

GAMBLING

I would hate to see legalized gambling in
California, nor do I favor a lottery. We ought to
finance the state by the strength of our people
and not by their weakness.

Ronald Reagan

It doesn't say much for society, if gambling is the
main method of raising money for good causes.

Bertram Troy

GARDEN

I have never had so many good ideas day after
day as when I worked in the garden.

John Erskine

GENEROSITY

What seems to be generosity is often no more than disguised ambition, which overlooks a small interest in order to secure a great one.

François de la Rochefoucauld

GENIUS

Men give me some credit for genius. All the genius I have lies just in this: When I have a subject in hand, I study it profoundly. Day and night it is before me. I explore it in all its bearings. My mind becomes pervaded with it. Then the effort which I make the people are pleased to call the fruit of genius. It is the fruit of labor and thought.

Alexander Hamilton

No great genius is without an admixture of madness.

Aristotle

GENTLEMAN

This is the final test of a gentleman: his respect for those who can be of no possible service to him.

William Lyon Phelps

GIVE

It is more blessed to give than to receive.

Acts 20:35

GIVING

God loveth a cheerful giver.

2 Corinthians 9:7

We make a living by what we get, but we make a life by what we give.

Norman MacEwan

He who waits to do a great deal of good at once, will never do anything.

Samuel Johnson

If there be any truer measure of a man than by what he does, it must be by what he gives.

Robert South

As the purse is emptied, the heart is filled.

Victor Hugo

GLORY

Real glory springs from the silent conquest of ourselves.

Joseph P. Thompson

GLUTTON

The fool that eats till he is sick must fast till he is well.

George W. Thornbury

Their kitchen is their shrine, the cook their priest, the table their altar, and their belly their god.

Charles Buck

GOALS

It must be borne in mind that the tragedy of life doesn't lie in not reaching your goal. The tragedy lies in having no goal to reach. It isn't a calamity to die with dreams unfulfilled, but it is a calamity to not dream. It is not a disgrace not to reach the stars, but it is a disgrace to have no stars to reach for. Not failure, but low aim, is sin.

Helmut Schmidt

Losers always concentrate on activities, but high achievers concentrate on planning and making every moment count in their efforts to reach progressively higher intermediate goals.

John R. Noe

In great attempts it is glorious even to fail.

Vince Lombardi

With no ideas of diamonds, we settle for glass.

Aim at the sun, and you may not reach it; but your arrow will fly far higher than if aimed at an object on a level with yourself.

Joel Hawes

He who aims at the moon may hit the top of a tree; he who aims at the top of a tree is unlikely to get off the ground.

GOD

God is our refuge and strength, a very present help in trouble. Therefore we will not fear.

Psalm 46:1,2

God is not a cosmic bellboy for whom we can press a button to get things.

Harry Emerson Fosdick

Two men please God: who serves Him with all his heart because he knows Him; who seeks Him with all his heart because he knows Him not.

Nikita Ivanovich Panin

It is only from the belief of the goodness and wisdom of a supreme being, that our calamities can be borne in the manner which becomes a man.

Henry Mackenzie

In what way, or by what manner of working God changes a soul from evil to good—how he impregnates the barren rock with priceless gems and gold—is, to the human mind, an impenetrable mystery.

Samuel Taylor Coleridge

We have been the recipients of the choicest bounties of heaven; we have been preserved these many years in peace and prosperity; we have grown in number, wealth, and power as no other nation has ever grown. But we have forgotten God! Intoxicated with unbroken success, we have become too self-sufficient to feel the necessity of redeeming and preserving grace, too proud to pray to the God who made us.

Abraham Lincoln

Belief in and dependence on God is absolutely essential. It will be an integral part of our public life as long as I am governor.

Ronald Reagan

GOD'S WILL

It is so. It cannot be otherwise.

Everything comes gradually and at its
appointed hour.

Ovid

GOLD

Gold is tested by fire; people are tested by gold.

GOOD

The world is sown with good; but unless I turn my
glad thoughts into practical living and till my own
field, I cannot reap a kernel of the good.

Helen Keller

Do all the good you can, in all the ways you can,
to all the souls you can, in every place you can, at
all the times you can, with all the zeal you can, as
long as ever you can.

John Wesley

GOOD BREEDING

Good breeding consists in concealing how much
we think of ourselves and how little we think of
other persons.

Mark Twain

GOOD NATURE

An inexhaustible good nature is one of the most precious gifts of heaven, spreading itself like oil over the troubled sea of thought, and keeping the mind smooth and equable in the roughest weather.

Washington Irving

GOOD TEMPER

Of cheerfulness, or a good temper—the more it is spent, the more it remains.

Ralph Waldo Emerson

GOODWILL

Moral of the Work: in war, resolution; in defeat, defiance; in victory, magnanimity; in peace, goodwill.

Winston Churchill

GOSPEL

You are writing a gospel,
A chapter each day,
By deeds that you do,
By words that you say.
Men read what you write
Whether faithless or true.
Say! What is the gospel
According to you?

GOSSIP

Of every ten persons who talk about you,
nine will say something bad, and the tenth
will say something good in a bad way.

Antoine Rivarol

The only time people dislike gossip is
when you gossip about them.

Will Rogers

Gossip is always a personal confession
either of malice or imbecility.

Josiah Gilbert Holland

Whoever gossips to you will gossip about you.

Who brings a tale takes two away.

Avoid a questioner, for he is also a tattler.

Gossiping and lying go together.

Shun the inquisitive, for you will be sure to
find him leaky. Open ears do not keep
conscientiously what has been intrusted
to them, and a word once spoken flies,
never to be recalled.

Horace

Nobody will keep the thing he hears to
himself, and nobody will repeat just what he
hears and no more.

Seneca

GOVERNMENT

The marvel of all history is the patience with which men and women submit to burdens unnecessarily laid upon them by their governments.

William E. Borah

The government is the only known vessel that leaks from the top.

James Reston

If you feel you are too busy to take an interest in government, feel that getting mixed up in politics is beneath your dignity or bad for business, then at least take time for one thing: Teach your children to count foreign currency—they'll need to, with the inheritance you're leaving them.

Willard M. Wilson

The best of all governments is that which teaches us to govern ourselves.

Johann Wolfgang von Goethe

You cannot get blood from a stone, but you can get a government grant to try.

Louis Phillips

GRACE

The will of God will not take you where the grace of God cannot keep you.

You say grace before meals. All right. But I say grace before the concert and the opera, and grace before the play and pantomime, and grace before I open a book, and grace before sketching, painting, swimming, fencing, boxing, walking, playing, dancing, and grace before I dip the pen in the ink.

G.K. Chesterton

God appoints our graces to be nurses to other men's weakness.

Henry Ward Beecher

GRACEFUL EXIT

Few men of action have been able to make a graceful exit at the appropriate time.

Malcolm Muggeridge

GRATITUDE

Happiness cannot be traveled to, owned, earned, worn, or consumed. Happiness is the spiritual experience of living every minute with love, grace, and gratitude.

Denis Waitley

A merry heart maketh a cheerful countenance . . . he that is of a merry heart hath a continual feast.

Proverbs 15:13,15

The greatest saint in the world is not he who prays most or fasts most; it is not he who gives alms, or is most eminent for temperance, chastity, or justice. It is he who is most thankful to God.

William Law

Dwell upon the brightest parts in every prospect
. . . and strive to be pleased with the
present circumstances.

Abraham Tucker

Gratitude is one of the least articulate of the
emotions, especially when it is deep.

Felix Frankfurter

Thank God every morning when you get up that
you have something to do which must be done,
whether you like it or not.

Charles Kingsley

Next to ingratitude, the most painful thing
to bear is gratitude.

Henry Ward Beecher

This is the day which the Lord hath made,
we will rejoice and be glad in it.

Psalm 118:24

GRAVE

Tombs are the clothes of the dead. A grave
is but a plain suit; a rich monument is an
embroidered one.

Thomas Fuller

GRAVITY

It's a good thing there's gravity or else when
birds died, they'd stay where they were.

Steven Wright

GRATEFULNESS

God gave you a gift of 86,400 seconds today.
Have you used one to say "thank you"?

William A. Ward

GREATNESS

If any man seeks for greatness, let him forget
greatness and ask for truth, and he will find both.

Horace Mann

The price of greatness is responsibility.

Winston Churchill

GREED

In a great river, great fish are found; but take heed
lest you be drowned.

Every crowd has a silver lining.

Phineas Taylor Barnum

There is no fire like passion, no shark like
hatred, no snare like folly, and no
torrent like greed.

There are many things that we would
throw away, if we were not afraid that
others might pick them up.

Oscar Wilde

He that is greedy of gain troubleth
his own house.

Proverbs 15:27

GRIEF

There is no grief which time does not
lessen and soften.

Cicero

The only cure for grief is action.

George Henry Lewes

The greatest griefs are those we
cause ourselves.

Sophocles

Patience, says another, is an excellent remedy
for grief, but submission to the hand of Him
that sends it is far better.

Charles Simmons

We should publish our joys and
conceal our griefs.

GROWTH

Undertake something that is difficult; it will do
you good. Unless you try to do something
beyond what you have already mastered,
you will never grow.

Ronald E. Osborn

If we don't change, we don't grow. If we don't
grow, we are not really living. Growth demands
a temporary surrender of security.

Gail Sheehy

A man is not old as long as he is
seeking something.

Jean Rostand

GUEST

The first day, a guest; the second, a burden; the third, a pest.

Edoudard R. Laboulaye

GUILT

A guilty conscience needs no accuser.

Fear is the tax that conscience pays to guilt.

George Sewell

It is base to filch a purse, daring to embezzle a million, but it is great beyond measure to steal a crown. The sin lessens as the guilt increases.

Johann von Schiller

Suspicion always haunts the guilty mind.

William Shakespeare

From the body of one guilty deed a thousand ghostly fears and haunting thoughts proceed.

William Wordsworth

GUTS

One of man's finest qualities is described by the simple word "guts"—the ability to take it. If you have the discipline to stand fast when your body wants to run, if you can control your temper and remain cheerful in the face of monotony or disappointment, you have "guts" in the soldiering sense.

Colonel John S. Roosman

HABIT

Habit, if not resisted, soon
becomes necessity.

Augustine of Hippo

The mind unlearns with difficulty what has
long been impressed on it.

Seneca

We are what we repeatedly do. Excellence,
then, is not an act, but a habit.

Aristotle

The unfortunate thing about this world is
that the good habits are much easier
to give up than the bad ones.

W. Somerset Maugham

HALFTIME

On Thanksgiving Day, all over America,
families sit down to dinner at the same
moment: halftime.

HANDICAPS

I thank God for my handicaps, for through them,
I have found myself, my work, and my God.

Helen Keller

HANGING

There is no man so good who, were he to submit
all his thoughts and actions to the law, would not
deserve hanging ten times in his life.

Michel Eyquem de Montaigne

HAPPINESS

One is happy as a result of one's own
efforts—once one knows the necessary
ingredients of happiness: simple tastes, a certain
degree of courage, self-denial to a point, love of
work, and, above all, a clear conscience.

George Sand

Everyone, without exception, is searching
for happiness.

Blaise Pascal

True happiness may be sought, thought, or
caught, but never bought.

When one door of happiness closes, another
opens, but often we look so long at the closed
door that we do not see the one that has
been opened for us.

Helen Keller

Happiness is good health and a bad memory.

Ingrid Bergman

Happiness is the only thing you can give without having.

All who would win joy, must share it; happiness was born a twin.

Lord Byron

All men have happiness as their object; there are no exceptions. However different the means they employ, they aim at the same end.

Blaise Pascal

Scatter seeds of kindness
everywhere you go;
Scatter bits of courtesy—watch
them grow and grow.
Gather buds of friendship, keep
them till full-blown;
You will find more happiness than
you have ever known.

Amy R. Raabe

Happiness is the natural flower of duty.

Phillips Brooks

No one is happy all his life long.

Euripides

Happiness is like a cat. If you try to coax it
or call it, it will avoid you. It will never come.
But if you pay no attention to it and go about your
business, you'll find it rubbing against your legs
and jumping into your lap.

William Bennett

The grand essentials of happiness are something to do, something to love, and something to hope for.

Happiness isn't something you experience; it's something you remember.

Oscar Levant

Happiness walks on busy feet.

Kitte Turmell

The really happy man is one who can enjoy the scenery on a detour.

Happiness comes of the capacity to feel deeply, to enjoy simply, to think freely, to risk life, to be needed

Storm Jamesom

We are all happy, if we only knew it.

Fyodor Dostoyevsky

Many a person seems to think it isn't enough for the government to guarantee him the pursuit of happiness. He insists it also run interference for him.

May we never let the things we can't have, or don't have, or shouldn't have, spoil our enjoyment of the things we do have and can have. As we value our happiness, let us not forget it, for one of the greatest lessons in life is learning to be happy without the things we cannot or should not have.

Richard L. Evans

Whoever is happy will make others happy, too.

Anne Frank

Those only are happy who have their minds on some object other than their own happiness . . . on the happiness of others . . . on the improvement of mankind . . . even on some art or pursuit, followed not as a means, but as itself an "ideal end."

When a man is happy he does not hear the clock strike.

HARVEST

Those who have not sown anything during their responsible life will have nothing to reap in the future.

George Gurdjieff

Whatsoever a man soweth, that shall he also reap.

Galatians 6:7

And let us not be weary in well doing: for in due season we shall reap, if we faint not.

Galatians 6:9

HASTE

Some persons do first, think afterward, and then repent forever.

Thomas Secker

A word and a stone let go cannot be called back.

Thomas Fuller

HATE

Hate is a prolonged form of suicide.

Douglas V. Steere

Whom they have injured, they also hate.

Marcus Annaeus Seneca

HEALTH

If we could give every individual the right
amount of nourishment and exercise, not too
little and not too much, we would have
found the safest way to health.

Hippocrates

Half the spiritual difficulties that men and women
suffer arise from a morbid state of health.

Henry Ward Beecher

HEART

Two things are bad for the heart—running up stairs
and running down people.

Bernard M. Baruch

The heart of a fool is in his mouth, but the mouth
of the wise man is in his heart.

Benjamin Franklin

He did it with all his heart, and prospered.

2 Chronicles 31:21

HEAVEN

If I ever reach heaven I expect to find three
wonders there: first, to meet some I had not
thought to see there; second to miss some I had
expected to see there; and third, the greatest
wonder of all, to find myself there.

John Newton

HELL

There may be some doubt about hell beyond
the grave but there is no doubt about there being
one on this side of it.

Ed Howe

HELP

Time and money spent in helping men to do more
for themselves is far better than mere giving.

Henry Ford

Two thirds of help is to give courage.

You cannot help men permanently by
doing for them what they could and should
do for themselves.

Abraham Lincoln

In about the same degree as you are helpful,
you will be happy.

Karl Reiland

Men are made stronger on realization that the helping hand they need is at the end of their own arm.

Sidney J. Phil

HERO

Show me a hero and I will write you a tragedy.

F. Scott Fitzgerald

HEROISM

The world's battlefields have been in the heart chiefly; more heroism has been displayed in the household and the closet, than on the most memorable battlefields in history.

Henry Ward Beecher

HISTORY

The main thing is to make history, not to write it.

Otto von Bismark

History never looks like history when you are living through it. It always looks confusing and messy, and it always feels uncomfortable.

John W. Gardner

HOLINESS

A true love of God must begin with a delight in his holiness.

Jonathan Edwards

Nothing can make a man truly great but being truly good, and partaking of God's holiness.

Matthew Henry

HOLY LIFE

The serene, silent beauty of a holy life is the most powerful influence in the world, next to the might of the Spirit of God.

Blaise Pascal

HOME

Kids won't roam if they're proud of their home.

A man travels the world over in search of what he needs and returns home to find it.

George Moore

HONESTY

Make yourself an honest man, and then you may be sure there is one less rascal in the world.

Thomas Carlyle

It is a shameful and unseemly thing to think one thing and speak another, but how odious to write one thing and think another.

Seneca

Honesty has come to mean the privilege of insulting you to your face without expecting redress.

Judith Martin

Never give 'em more than one barrel to start with.
But if they are foolish enough to ask for more,
then give 'em the other barrel right
between the eyes.

John Wesley Dafoe

Honesty is one part of eloquence. We persuade
others by being in earnest ourselves.

William Hazlitt

Honesty is a fine jewel, but much out of fashion.

Honest criticism is hard to take, particularly from a
relative, a friend, an acquaintance, or a stranger.

Franklin P. Jones

HONOR

Show me the man you honor, and I will
know what kind of a man you are, for it shows
me what your ideal of manhood is, and what kind
of a man you long to be.

Thomas Carlyle

If honor be your clothing, the suit will last a
lifetime; but if clothing be your honor, it
will soon be worn threadbare.

William Arnot

HOPE

Hope is a waking dream.

Aristotle

Now the God of hope fill you with all joy and peace in believing, that ye may abound in hope.

Romans 15:13

Oh, what a valiant faculty is hope.

Michel de Montaigne

Hope is grief's best music.

There is one thing which gives radiance to everything. It is the idea of something around the corner.

G.K. Chesterton

Hope is itself a species of happiness, and, perhaps, the chief happiness which this world affords.

Samuel Johnson

There is no medicine like hope, no incentive so great, and no tonic so powerful as expectation of something tomorrow.

Orison Swett Marden

They sailed. They sailed. Then spoke the mate:
"This mad sea shows its teeth tonight
He curls his lip, he lies in wait,
With lifted teeth, as if to bite!
Brave admiral, say but one good word:
What shall we do when hope is gone?"
The words leapt like a leaping sword:
"Sail on! sail on! and on!"

HOSTS

People are either born hosts or born guests.

Sir Max Beerbohm

HOUSEWORK

I hate housework! You make the beds, you
do the dishes, and six months later you
have to start all over again.

Joan Rivers

HUMAN SPIRIT

The human spirit is stronger than anything
that can happen to it.

George C. Scott

HUMILITY

A humble person is not himself conscious
of his humility. Truth and the like perhaps admit of
measurement, but not humility. Inborn humility
can never remain hidden, and yet the possessor
is unaware of its existence.

Mahatma Gandhi

It is no great thing to be humble when you are
brought low; but to be humble when you are
praised is a great and rare attainment.

Bernard of Clairvaux

To be humble to superiors, is duty; to equals, is
courtesy; to inferiors, is nobleness; and to all,
safety; it being a virtue that, for all its lowliness,
commandeth those it stoops to.

Thomas Moore

There is no quality of human nature so nearly
royal as the ability to yield gracefully.

Charles Conrad

HUMOR

The world is a perpetual caricature of itself; at
every moment it is the mockery and the
contradiction of what it is pretending to be.
But as it nevertheless intends all the time to
be something different and highly dignified,
at the next moment it corrects and checks and
tries to cover up the absurd thing it was; so that a
conventional world, a world of masks, is
superimposed on the reality, and passes in
every sphere of human interest for the reality
itself. Humor is the perception of this illusion,
whilst the convention continues to be maintained,
as if we had not observed its absurdity.

George Santayana

If you could choose one characteristic that would
get you through life, choose a sense of humor.

Jennifer James

The secret source of humor is not joy but sorrow.

Mark Twain

Whenever you find humor, you find
pathos close by his side.

Edwin Percy Whipple

Humor is the instinct for taking pain playfully.

Max Eastman

If I had no sense of humor, I should long ago
have committed suicide.

Mahatma Gandhi

A cardinal rule of humor: Never say anything
about anyone that the person can't change in five
seconds. Use the AT&T test for stories and
jokes: make sure it's Appropriate,
Timely, and Tasteful.

Susan RoAne

Against the assault of humor,
nothing can stand.

Mark Twain

The man who has had the job I've had and didn't
have a sense of humor wouldn't still be here.

Harry Truman

I think the next best thing to solving a problem
is finding some humor in it.

Frank A. Clark

HUSBAND

A good husband makes a good wife.

IDEALS

Ideals are like the stars: we never reach them,
but like the mariners of the sea, we chart our
course by them.

Carl Schurz

IDEAS

A new idea is delicate. It can be killed by a
sneer or a yawn; it can be stabbed to death
by a quip and worried to death by a frown
on the right man's brow.

Charles Brower

Almost all new ideas have a certain aspect of
foolishness when they are first produced.

Alfred North Whitehead

Ideas are like rabbits. You get a couple
and learn how to handle them, and pretty
soon you have a dozen.

Ideas lose themselves as quickly as quail, and
one must wing them the minute they raise out of
the grass or they are gone.

Thomas Kennedy

IDLENESS

It is impossible to enjoy idling thoroughly
unless one has plenty of work to do.

Jerome K. Jerome

IDOL

A God who let us prove his existence
would be an idol.

Dietrich Bonhoeffer

IGNORANCE

It is profound ignorance that inspires
the dogmatic tone.

It takes a lot of things to prove you are smart,
but only one thing to prove you are ignorant.

Don Herold

ILL WIND

It is an ill wind that blows when you
leave the hairdresser.

Phyllis Diller

IMAGINATION

Sometimes I've believed as many as six
impossible things before breakfast.

Lewis Carroll

IMITATE

When people are free to do as they please,
they usually imitate each other.

Eric Hoffer

IMMORTALITY

If your contribution has been vital there will
always be somebody to pick up where you left
off, and that will be your claim to immortality.

Walter Gropius

IMPATIENCE

I have not so great a struggle with my vices,
great and numerous as they are, as I have with
my impatience. My efforts are not absolutely
useless; yet I have never been able to conquer
this ferocious wild beast.

John Calvin

IMPORTANCE

Almost every man you meet feels himself
superior to you in some way; and a sure way
to his heart is to let him realize that you
recognize his importance.

Dale Carnegie

IMPORTANT MOMENTS

One doesn't recognize in one's life the really
important moments—not until it's too late.

Agatha Christie

IMPULSE

Since the generality of persons act from impulse much more than from principle, men are neither so good nor so bad as we are apt to think them.

Augustus and Julius Hare

INADEQUACIES

The higher the ape goes, the more he shows his tail.

INCOME TAX

The hardest thing in the world to understand is income tax.

Albert Einstein

INDUSTRY

If you have great talents, industry will improve them; if moderate abilities, industry will supply their deficiencies. Nothing is denied to well-directed labor; nothing is ever to be attained without it.

Joshua Reynolds

In the ordinary business of life, industry can do anything which genius can do, and very many things which it cannot.

Henry Ward Beecher

A man who gives his children habits of industry provides for them better than by giving them a fortune.

Richard Whatley

No thoroughly occupied man was ever
yet very miserable.

Letitla Landon

Industry keeps the body healthy, the mind clear,
the heart whole, and the purse full.

Charles Simmons

Industry need not wish, and he that lives upon
hopes will die fasting. There are no gains
without pains. He that hath a trade hath an
estate, and he that hath a calling hath an office of
profit and honor; but then the trade must be
worked at, and the calling followed, or neither the
estate nor the office will enable us to pay our
taxes. If we are industrious, we shall never starve;
for, at the workingman's house hunger looks in,
but dares not enter. Nor will the bailiff or the
constable enter, for industry pays debts, while
idleness and neglect increase them.

Benjamin Franklin

INFERIORITY

No man who says, "I'm as good as you," believes
it. He would not say it if he did. The Saint Bernard
never says it to the toy dog, nor the scholar to the
dunce, nor the employable to the bum, nor the
pretty woman to the plain. The claim to equality is
made only by those who feel themselves to be in
some way inferior. What it expresses is the
itching, smarting awareness of an inferiority
which the patient refuses to accept,
and therefore resents.

C.S. Lewis

INFIDEL

It is always safe to follow the religious belief that our mother taught us; there never was a mother yet who taught her child to be an infidel.

Henry Wheeler Shaw

INFIDELITY

The nurse of infidelity is sensuality.

Richard Cecil

Man may doubt here and there, but mankind does not doubt. The universal conscience is larger than the individual conscience, and that constantly comes in to correct and check our infidelity.

Hugh Reginald Haweis

INFLUENCE

I really believe that more harm is done by old men who cling to their influence than by young men who anticipate it.

Owen D. Young

INGENUITY

Ingenuity is required even for the practice of vice.

INGRATITUDE

Ingratitude is always a form of weakness. I have never known a man of real ability to be ungrateful.

Johann Wolfgang von Goethe

INHERITANCE

Never say you know a man till you have
divided an inheritance with him.

Johann Kaspar Lavater

INJURY

The injury we do and the one we suffer are not
weighed in the same scale.

INJUSTICE

Those who commit injustice bear the
greatest burden.

Hosea Ballou

INNOCENCE

Innocence is a desirable thing, a dainty thing, an
appealing thing, in its place; but carried too far, it
is merely ridiculous.

Dorothy Parker

No protection is as sure as innocence.

INNOVATOR

The entrepreneur finds a need and fills it. The
innovator anticipates or creates
a need and fills it.

Denis E. Waitley and Robert B. Tucker

INQUIRY

Let not the freedom of inquiry be shackled. If it multiplies contentions among the wise and virtuous, it exercises the charity of those who contend. If it shakes for a time the belief that is rested only on prejudice, it finally settles it on the broader and more solid basis of conviction.

Henry Kirke White

INSANITY

Insanity is often the logic of an accurate mind overtaxed.

Oliver Wendell Holmes

INSIGHT

Though you may see another's back, you cannot see your own.

INSINCERITY

Nothing is more disgraceful than insincerity.

Cicero

INSPIRATION

Inspirations never go in for long engagements; they demand immediate marriage to action.

Brendan Francis

INSTINCT

Trust your own instinct. Your mistakes might as well be your own, instead of someone else's.

Billy Wilder

INSULT

Whatever be the motive of an insult it is always best to overlook it; for folly scarcely can deserve resentment, and malice is punished by neglect.

Samuel Johnson

There are two insults no human being will endure: that he has no sense of humor, and that he has never known trouble.

Sinclair Lewis

A graceful taunt is worth a thousand insults.

Louis Nizer

INSURANCE

Insurance: Something that keeps you poor all your life so that you can die rich.

INTEGRITY

Integrity is the glue that holds our way of life together.

Billy Graham

INTELLECT

The more we know of any one ground of
knowledge, the further we see into the
general domains of intellect.

(James Henry) Leigh Hunt

INTELLECTUAL

An intellectual is a man who takes more words
than necessary to tell more than he knows.

Dwight D. Eisenhower

INTEREST

Our delight in any particular study, art, or science
rises and improves in proportion to the application
which we bestow upon it. Thus, what was at first
an exercise becomes at length an entertainment.

Joseph Addison

What we love to do we find time to do.

John Lancaster Spalding

INTRODUCTIONS

Introductions. Nobody reads them. But our
editor said, "introduction?" And what he
says goes. This is it.

William Cole and Louis Phillips

INTUITION

Intuition is given only to him who has undergone
long preparation to receive it.

Louis Pasteur

Intuition is a spiritual faculty and does not
explain, but simply points the way.

Florence Scovel Shinn

INVENTING

Inventing is a combination of brains and
materials. The more brains you use,
the less materials you need.

Charles F. Kettering

Name the greatest of all the inventors: Accident.

Mark Twain

JEALOUSY

All jealousy must be strangled in its birth,
or time will soon make it strong enough to
overcome the truth.

Sir William Davenant

Anger and jealousy can no more bear to lose
sight of their objects than love.

George Eliot

Jealousy is . . . a tiger that tears not only its
prey but also its own raging heart.

Michael Beer

To jealousy, nothing is more frightful
than laughter.

Françoise Sagan

There is never jealousy where there is
not strong regard.

Washington Irving

There are no conditions to which a man cannot
become accustomed, especially if he sees that
all those around him live the same way.

Leo Tolstoy

Jealousy, that dragon which slays love under the pretence of keeping it alive.

Havelock Ellis

JOB

If you have a job without aggravations, you don't have a job.

Malcolm Forbes

JOKES

There are things of deadly earnest that can only be safely mentioned under cover of a joke.

J. J. Procter

Were it not for my little jokes, I could not bear the burdens of this office.

Abraham Lincoln

JOURNALISM

The sole aim of journalism should be service. The press is a great power, but just as an unchained torrent of water submerges the whole countryside and devastates crops, even so an uncontrolled pen serves but to destroy. If the control is from without, it proves more poisonous than want of control. It can be profitable only when exercised from within. If this line of reasoning is correct, how many of the journals in the world would stand the test? But who would stop those that are useless? And who should be the judge? The useful and the useless must, like good and evil generally, go on together, and man must make his choice.

Mahatma Gandhi

JOURNALISTS

Journalists do not live by words alone, although
sometimes they have to eat them.

Adlai Stevenson

JOY

The joy of the heart makes the face fair.

One joy scatters a hundred griefs.

Joy has nothing to do with material things, or with
a man's outward circumstance . . . a man living in
the lap of luxury can be wretched, and a man in
the depths of poverty can overflow with joy.

William Barclay

One filled with joy preaches without preaching.

Mother Teresa

Grief can take care of itself, but to get the
full value of joy you must have somebody
to divide it with.

Mark Twain

Joy is the flag you fly when the Prince of Peace is
in residence within your heart.

Wilfred Peterson

Joys divided are increased.

Josiah Gilbert Holland

JUDGE

Four things belong to a judge: to hear courteously, to answer wisely, to consider soberly, and to decide impartially.

Socrates

Judge not, that ye be not judged.

Matthew 7:1

JUDGMENT

It is well, when judging a friend, to remember that he is judging you with the same godlike and superior impartiality.

Arnold Bennett

Take each man's censure, but reserve thy judgment.

William Shakespeare

JUSTICE

Justice and power must be brought together, so that whatever is just may be powerful, and whatever is powerful may be just.

Blaise Pascal

I tremble for my country when I reflect that God is just.

Thomas Jefferson

We need to rectify this mockery of justice and seek to realign the imbalanced scales of justice that all too often subjugate the rights and safety of society to the privileged exploitations and atrocities by the criminal.

John L. McClellan

Faith in the ability of a leader is of slight service unless it be united with faith in his justice.

George Washington Goethals

Justice is the great interest of man on earth. It is the ligament which holds civilized beings and civilized nations together. Wherever her temple stands, and so long as it is duly honored, there is a foundation for social security, general happiness, and the improvement and progress of our race. And whoever labors on this edifice with usefulness and distinction, whoever clears its foundations, strengthens its pillars, adorns its entablatures, or contributes to raise its august dome still higher in the skies, connects himself, in name, and fame, and character, with that which is and must be as durable as the frame of human society.

Daniel Webster

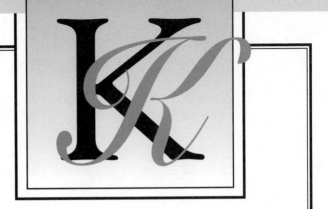

KINDNESS

A kind heart is a fountain of gladness, making everything in its vicinity freshen into smiles.

Washington Irving

The greatness of a man can nearly always be measured by his willingness to be kind.

G. Young

Kindness is in our power, even when fondness is not.

Samuel Johnson

Human kindness has never weakened the stamina or softened the fiber of a free people. A nation does not have to be cruel in order to be tough.

Franklin Delano Roosevelt

Kindness consists in loving people more than they deserve.

Joseph Joubert

One of the most difficult things to give away is kindness—it is usually returned.

The cheapest of all things is kindness, its exercise
requiring the least possible trouble
and self-sacrifice.

Samuel Smiles

A more glorious victory cannot be gained over
another man, than this: that when the injury began
on his part, the kindness should begin on ours.

John Tillotson

Kind words can be short and easy to speak,
but their echoes are truly endless.

Mother Teresa

KINGS

Kings and such are just as funny as politicians.

KISS

It is the passion that is in a kiss that gives to
it its sweetness; it is the affection in a kiss
that sanctifies it.

Christian Nestell Bovee

The sound of a kiss is not so loud as that of a
cannon, but its echo lasts a great deal longer.

Oliver Wendell Holmes

KNOW-IT-ALL

He who has no inclination to learn more will be
very apt to think that he knows enough.

Sir John Powell

KNOWLEDGE

He knows so little and knows it so fluently.

Ellen Anderson Gholson Glasgow

The more extensive a man's knowledge of what has been done, the greater will be his power of knowing what to do.

Benjamin Disraeli

One half of knowing what you want is knowing what you must give up before you get it.

Sidney Howard

All wish to possess knowledge, but few, comparatively speaking, are willing to pay the price.

Juvenal

If you have knowledge, let others light their candles at it.

Thomas Fuller

Strange how much you've got to know before you know how little you know.

Know thyself? If I knew myself, I'd run away.

Johann Wolfgang von Goethe

Know yourself. Don't accept your dog's admiration as conclusive evidence that you are wonderful.

Ann Landers

LABOR

If you would relish food, labor for it before you take it; if enjoy clothing, pay for it before you wear it; if you would sleep soundly, take a clear conscience to bed with you.

Benjamin Franklin

God sells us all things at the price of labor.

Leonardo da Vinci

LAST BREATH

Each person is born to one possession which outvalues all the others: his last breath.

Mark Twain

LAUGHTER

A laugh is a smile that bursts.

Mary H. Waldrip

No one is laughable who laughs
at himself.

Seneca

No one is more profoundly sad than he
who laughs too much.

Jean Paul Richter

If you wish to glimpse inside a human soul and
get to know a man, don't bother analyzing his
ways of being silent, of talking, of weeping, or
seeing how much he is moved by noble ideas;
you'll get better results if you just watch him laugh.
If he laughs well, he's a good man.

Fyodor Dostoyevsky

With the fearful strain that is on me night and day,
if I did not laugh I should die.

Abraham Lincoln

Laughter is like changing a baby's diaper: it
doesn't permanently solve any problems, but it
makes things more acceptable for a while.

Of all the things God created, I am often most
grateful he created laughter.

Charles Swindoll

LAW

Laws are like sausages. It is better not to see
them being made.

Otto von Bismark

LAWSUIT

I was never ruined but twice—once when I lost a
lawsuit, once when I won one.

Voltaire

Win your lawsuit and lose your money.

LAWYER

Here's an amazing story: A man in Orlando, Florida, was hit by eight cars in a row and only one stopped. The first seven drivers thought he was a lawyer. The eighth was a lawyer.

Jay Leno

LAZINESS

Laziness travels so slowly that poverty soon overtakes him.

Benjamin Franklin

Laziness is a secret ingredient that goes into failure. But it's only kept a secret from the person who fails.

Robert Half

Some people wait so long for their ship to come in, their pier collapses.

John Goddard

LEADERSHIP

Where the chief walks, there questions are decided.

The final test of a leader is that he leaves behind him in other men the conviction and the will to carry on.

Walter Lippmann

Learning is the essential fuel for the leader, the source of high-octane energy that keeps up the momentum by continually sparking new understanding, new ideas, and new challenges. It is absolutely indispensable under today's conditions of rapid change and complexity. Very simply, those who do not learn do not long survive as leaders.

Warren Bennis and Burt Nanus

The ulimate responsibility of a leader is to facilitate other people's development as well as his own.

Fred Pryor

The first responsibility of a leader is to define reality. The last is to say thank you. In between the leader is a servant.

Max Dupree

A leader is a dealer in hope.

Napoleon

Leaders have two important characteristics: first, they are going somewhere; second, they are able to persuade other people to go with them.

We expect our leaders to be better than we are . . . and they should be—or why are we following them?

Paul Harvey

It is said that if Noah's ark had had to be built by a company, they would not have laid the keel yet; and it may be so. What is many men's business is nobody's business. The greatest things are accomplished by individual men.

Charles Haddon Spurgeon

Leadership is a word and a concept that has been more argued than almost any other I know. I am not one of the desk-pounding type that likes to stick out his jaw and look like he is bossing the show. I would far rather get behind and recognizing the frailties and the requirements of human nature, I would rather try to persuade a man to go along, because once I have persuaded him he will stick. If I scare him, he will stay just as long as he is scared, and then he is gone.

Dwight David Eisenhower

He that commands well shall be obeyed well.

Two captains sink a ship.

An army of a thousand is easy to find, but, ah, how difficult to find a general.

LEARNING

I've known countless people who were reservoirs of learning yet never had a thought.

Wilson Mizner

Seeing much, suffering much and studying much, are the three pillars of learning.

Benjamin Disraeli

Wear your learning, like your watch, in a private pocket. Do not pull it out merely to show that you have one. If asked what o'clock it is, tell it; but do not proclaim it hourly and unasked, like the watchman.

Lord Chesterfield

LENDING

Lending is like throwing away; being paid is like finding something.

LETTERS

One of the pleasures of reading old letters is the knowledge that they need no answer.

Lord Byron

Sir, more than kisses, letters mingle souls; for, thus friends absent speak.

John Donne

LIBERTY

Still, if you will not fight for the right when you can easily win without bloodshed; if you will not fight when your victory will be sure and not too costly, you may come to the moment when you will have a fight with all the odds against you and only a precarious chance of survival. There may even be a worse case. You may have to fight when there is no hope of victory, because it is better to perish than live as slaves.

Winston Churchill

Every man has a property in his own person; this nobody has a right to but himself.

John Locke

If we mean to support the liberty and independence which have cost us so much blood and treasure to establish, we must drive far away the demon of party spirit and local reproach.

George Washington

They that can give up essential liberty to obtain a little temporary safety, deserve neither liberty nor safety.

Benjamin Franklin

LIES

He that once deceives, is ever suspected.

Sin has many tools, but a lie is the handle that fits them all.

Oliver Wendell Holmes

He who tells a lie is not sensible how great a task he undertakes; for he must be forced to invent twenty more to maintain one.

Alexander Pope

One of the striking differences between a cat and a lie is that a cat has only nine lives.

Mark Twain

He that will lie, will steal. One deceit needs many others, and so the whole house is built in the air and must soon come to the ground.

Baltasar Gracian

You can best reward a liar by believing nothing of what he says.

Aristippus

Show me a liar, and I will show you a thief.

Half a fact is a whole falsehood. He who gives the truth a false coloring by his false manner of telling it, is the worst of liars.

Elias Lyman Magoon

Lying to ourselves is more deeply ingrained than lying to others.

Fyoder Dostoyevsky

LIFE

Live mindful of how brief your life is.

Horace

Life happens at the level of events, not words.

Alfred Adler

Do not take life too seriously; you will never get out of it alive.

Elbert Hubbard

Avoiding danger is no safer in the long run than outright exposure. Life is either a daring adventure, or nothing.

Helen Keller

The measure of life is not its duration, but its donation.

Peter Marshall

The mere sense of living is joy enough.

Emily Dickinson

Life does not cease to be funny when people die any more than it ceases to be serious when people laugh.

George Bernard Shaw

Life is something to do when you can't get to sleep.

Fran Lebowitz

Life is a great canvas, and you should throw all the paint on it you can.

Danny Kaye

Life is always at some turning point.

Irwin Edman

I like living. I have sometimes been wildly, despairingly, acutely miserable, racked with sorrow, but through it all I still know quite certainly that just to be alive is a grand thing.

Agatha Christie

Life is what happens to you while you're making other plans.

Robert Balzer

Every day is a little life, and our whole life is but a day repeated. Therefore live every day as if it would be the last. Those that dare lose a day, are dangerously prodigal; those that dare misspend it are desperate.

Joseph Hall

The secret of long life is double careers. One to about age sixty, then another for the next thirty years.

David Ogilvy

LIMITATIONS

The man with insight enough to admit his limitations comes nearest to perfection.

Johann Wolfgang von Goethe

Imposing limitations on yourself is cowardly because it protects you from having to try, and perhaps failing.

Vladimir Zworykin

LITTLE THINGS

Enjoy the little things, for one day you may look back and realize they were the big things.

Robert Brault

LONELINESS

The worst loneliness is not to be comfortable with yourself.

Mark Twain

LONGSUFFERING

Strength is born in the deep silence of longsuffering hearts, not amidst joy.

Felicia Dorothea Browne Hemans

LOS ANGELES

The difference between Los Angeles and yogurt is that yogurt has real culture.

Tom Taussik

LOVE

Hatred stirreth up strifes: but love
covereth all sins.

Proverbs 10:12

Love makes one fit for any work.

Faith, like light, should always be simple and
unbending; while love, like warmth, should beam
forth on every side and bend to every necessity
of our brethren.

Martin Luther

Perfect love casteth out fear.

1 John 4:18

Those who love deeply never grow old; they
may die of old age, but they die young.

Sir Arthur Wing Pinero

Greater love hath no man than this, that a man
lay down his life for his friends.

John 15:13

The way to love anything is to realize
that it might be lost.

G. K. Chesterton

LOYALTY

Loyalty means nothing unless it has at its heart
the absolute principle of self-sacrifice.

Thomas Woodrow Wilson

Unless you can find some sort of loyalty, you cannot find unity and peace in your active living.

Josiah Royce

My kind of loyalty was loyalty to one's country, not to its institutions or its officeholders. The country is the real thing, the substantial thing, the eternal thing; it is the thing to watch over, and care for, and be loyal to.

Mark Twain

LUCK

Luck sometimes visits a fool, but never sits down with him.

Depend on the rabbit's foot if you will, but it didn't work for the rabbit.

LUST

Lust is an enemy to the purse, a foe to the person, a canker to the mind, a corrosive to the conscience, a weakness of the wit, a besotter of the senses, and, finally, a mortal bane to all the body.

Pliny the Elder

MADNESS

When we remember we are all mad, the
mysteries disappear and life stands explained.

Mark Twain

MALICE

Malice swallows the greater part of
its own venom.

Publilius Syrus

MANHOOD

There is no miraculous change that takes place
in a boy that makes him a man. He becomes a
man by being a man.

Louis L'Amour

Manliness consists not in bluff, bravado, or
lordliness. It consists in daring to do the right
and facing consequences, whether it is in
matters social, political, or other. It consists in
deeds, not in words.

Mahatma Gandhi

MANNERS

Manners are a sensitive awareness of the feelings of others. If you have that awareness, you have good manners, no matter what fork you use.

Emily Post

Good manners and good morals are sworn friends and fast allies.

Cyrus Augustus Bartol

Good manners and soft words have brought many a difficult thing to pass.

Sir John Vanbrugh

MANUAL LABOR

Manual labor to my father was not only good and decent for its own sake, but as he was given to saying, it straightened out one's thoughts.

Mary Ellen Chase

MARMALADE

I got the blues thinking of the future, so I left off and made some marmalade. It's amazing how it cheers one up to shred oranges and scrub the floor.

D.H. Lawrence

MARRIAGE

Men dream in courtship, but in wedlock wake.

Alexander Pope

A successful marriage is an edifice that must be rebuilt every day.

Andre Maurois

Marriage is the greatest educational institution on earth.

Channing Pollock

The great secret of a successful marriage is to treat all disasters as incidents and none of the incidents as disasters.

Harold Nicholson

Marriage with a good woman is a harbor in the tempest of life; with a bad woman, it is a tempest in the harbor.

John Petit-Senn

MATURITY

To be mature means to face, and not evade, every fresh crisis that comes.

Fritz Kunkel

The way of a superior man is three-fold: virtuous, he is free from anxieties; wise, he is free from perplexities; bold, he is free from fear.

Confucius

It is the mark of a superior man that, left to himself, he is able endlessly to amuse, interest, and entertain himself out of his personal stock of meditations, ideas, criticisms, memories, philosophy, humor, and what not.

George Jean Nathan

MAYONNAISE

I always wanted to write a book that ended with the word mayonnaise.

Richard Brautigan

MEANING

He doesn't know the meaning of the word fear— but then again, he doesn't know the meaning of most words.

MEDITATION

If we are willing to spend hours on end to learn to play the piano, operate a computer, or fly an airplane, it is sheer nonsense for us to imagine that we can learn the high art of getting guidance through communion with the Lord without being willing to set aside time for it.

Paul Rees

Though reading and conversation may furnish us with many ideas of men and things, our own meditation must form our judgement.

Isaac Watts

MEEKNESS

Meekness is imperfect if it be not both active and passive, leading us to subdue our own passions and resentments, as well as to bear patiently the passions and resentments of others.

John Watson Foster

MEMORIES

Money can't buy happiness, but it will get you a
better class of memories.

Ronald Reagan

MEMORY

Memory is the diary we all carry about with us.

Oscar Wilde

Do not forget little kindnesses and do not remember small faults.

Memory is the cabinet of imagination, the treasury
of reason, the registry of conscience, and the
council chamber of thought.

Basil the Great

The secret of a good memory is attention, and
attention to a subject depends upon our interest in
it. We rarely forget that which has made a deep
impression on our minds.

Tryon Edwards

They teach us to remember; why do they not
teach us to forget? There is not a man living who
has not, some time in his life, admitted that
memory was as much of a curse as a blessing.

Francis Alexander Durivage

To be wronged is nothing unless you
continue to remember it.

Confucius

When I was younger, I could remember anything, whether it had happened or not; but my faculties are decaying now, and soon I shall be so that I cannot remember anything but the things that never happened. It is sad to go to pieces like this, but we all have to do it.

Mark Twain

A retentive memory is a good thing, but the ability to forget is the true token of greatness.

Elbert Hubbard

Recollection is the only paradise from which we cannot be turned out.

Jean Paul Richter

We forget all too soon the things we thought we could never forget.

Joan Didion

What was hard to bear is sweet to remember.

MERRY HEART

He that is of a merry heart hath a continual feast.

Proverbs 15:15

MIDAS TOUCH

She had the Midas touch. Everything she touched turned into a muffler.

Lisa Smerling

MIDDLE OF THE ROAD

Standing in the middle of the road is very
dangerous; you get knocked down by
traffic from both sides.

Margaret Thatcher

MIME

If you shoot a mime, should you use a silencer?

Steven Wright

MIND

A mind once cultivated will not lie fallow
for half an hour.

Edward G. Gulwer-Lytton

The mind is like the stomach. It is not how
much you put into it that counts, but how
much it digests.

Albert Jay Nock

If thou desirest ease, in the first place take care of
the ease of thy mind; for that will make all other
sufferings easy. But nothing can support a man
whose mind is wounded.

Thomas Fuller

The best of all things is to learn. Money can
be lost or stolen, health and strength may fail,
but what you have committed to your
mind is yours forever.

His mind is so open that the wind
whistles through it.

Heywood Broun

MIRROR

The world is like a mirror; frown at it, and it frowns
at you. Smile and it smiles, too.

Herbert Samuels

MISERY

Human misery must somewhere have a stop;
there is no wind that always blows a storm.

Euripides

Depend upon it, that if a man talks of his
misfortunes there is something in them that is not
disagreeable to him: for where there is nothing but
pure misery, there never is any mention of it.

Samuel Johnson

A misery is not to be measured from the nature of
the evil, but from the temper of the sufferer.

Joseph Addison

MISFORTUNE

Doing what's right is no guarantee against
misfortune.

William McFee

Misfortune arrives on horseback but
departs on foot.

Misfortunes find their way even on
the darkest night.

Most of our misfortunes are more supportable
than the comments of our friends upon them.

Charles Caleb Colton

It is well to treasure the memories of past misfortunes; they constitute our bank of fortitude.

Erick Hoffer

By speaking of our misfortunes we often seem to
get relief.

Pierre Corneille

If all misfortunes were laid in one common heap
whence everyone must take an equal portion,
most people would be contented to take
their own and depart.

Socrates

MISTAKES

Now what should happen when you make a
mistake is this: You take your knocks, you learn
your lessons, and then you move on. That's the
healthiest way to deal with a problem.

Ronald Reagan

A mistake only proves that someone stopped
talking long enough to do something.

Michael LeBoeuf

Any man may make a mistake, but none but a fool will continue in it.

Cicero

The only people who make no mistakes are dead people. I saw a man last week who has not made a mistake for four thousand years. He was a mummy in the Egyptian department of the British Museum.

Heman Lincoln Wayland

A just cause is not ruined by a few mistakes.

Fyodor Dostoyevsky

Learn from the mistakes of others—you can't live long enough to make them all yourself.

Martin Vanbee

It is very easy to forgive others their mistakes; it takes more grit and gumption to forgive them for having witnessed your own.

MISUNDERSTANDING

Nine-tenths of the serious controversies which arise in life result from misunderstanding.

Louis Dembitz Brandeis

MOB

A mob is the scum that rises upmost when the nation boils.

John Dryden

MODESTY

Modesty is the citadel of beauty and virtue.

Demades

Modesty is the color of virtue.

Diogenes

MONEY

Getting money is like digging with a needle;
spending it is like water soaking into sand.

If you marry for money only, you will
suffer . . . in comfort.

Dr. Murray Banks

No one would remember the Good Samaritan
if he'd only had good intentions. He had
money as well.

Margaret Thatcher

Make all you can, save all you can,
give all you can.

John Wesley

Our incomes are like our shoes: if too small,
they gall and pinch us; but if too large, they
cause us to stumble and to trip.

Charles Caleb Colton

By doing good with his money, a man, as it were,
stamps the image of God upon it, and makes it
pass current for the merchandise of heaven.

John Rutledge

MONSTERS

There are very few monsters who warrant
the fear we have of them.

Andre Gide

MORALITY

When you introduce a moral lesson let it be brief.

Horace

Let us with caution indulge the supposition that
morality can be maintained without religion.
Reason and experience both forbid us to expect
that national morality can prevail in exclusion of
religious principle.

George Washington

To give a man a full knowledge of true morality, I
would send him to no other book than the New
Testament.

John Locke

I have never found a thorough, pervading, en-
during morality but in those who feared God.

Friedrich Heinrich Jacobi

Every young man would do well to remember that
all successful business stands on the foundation
of morality.

Henry Ward Beecher

It is a wicked thing to be neutral between
right and wrong.

Theodore Roosevelt

MORAL LAW

No matter what theory of the origin of government
you adopt, if you follow it out to its legitimate
conclusions it will bring you face to face
with the moral law.

Henry van Dyke

MORNING

Weeping may endure for a night, but joy cometh
in the morning.

Psalm 30:5

MOTHER

Stories first heard at a mother's knee are never
wholly forgotten—a little spring that never quite
dries up in our journey through scorching years.

Giovanni Ruffini

An ounce of mother is worth a pound of clergy.

The mother's heart is the child's schoolroom.

Henry Ward Beecher

MOTHS

What really happened to the buffaloes is just what
you might expect if you've ever seen one in a
zoo—the moths got into them.

Will Cuppy

MOTIVES

Men are not only bad from good motives, but also often good from bad motives.

G. K. Chesterton

Man sees your actions, but God your motives.

Thomas à Kempis

Never ascribe to an opponent motives meaner than your own.

Sir James Matthew

MUSIC

Music is the art of the prophets, the only art that can calm the agitations of the soul; it is one of the most magnificent and delightful presents God has given us.

Martin Luther

Music is a discipline, and a mistress of order and good manners, she makes the people milder and gentler, more moral and more reasonable.

Martin Luther

NAME-DROPPER

I mustn't go singling out names. One must
not be a name-dropper, as Her Majesty
remarked to me yesterday.

Norman St. John Stevas

NARCISSIST

A narcissist is someone better-looking
than you are.

Gore Vidal

NEEDS

He who buys what he needs not, may
have to sell what he needs.

NEGLECT

Neglect will kill an injury sooner than revenge.

NEUROSIS

Work and love—these are the basics. Without
them there is neurosis.

Theodor Reik

NEWSPAPER

I fear three newspapers more than a hundred
thousand bayonets.

Napoleon Bonaparte

If newspapers are useful in overthrowing tyrants,
it is only to establish a tyranny of their own.

James Fenimore Cooper

NICKNAMES

Nicknames stick to people, and the most ridiculous are the most adhesive.

Thomas Chandler Haliburton

NO

One must have the courage to say "no," even at
the risk of displeasing others.

Fritz Kunkel

NONESSENTIALS

Besides the noble art of getting things done, there
is the noble art of leaving things undone. The
wisdom of life consists in the elimination of non-
essentials.

Lin Yutang

NOSTALGIA

Nostalgia: A device that removes the ruts and pot-
holes from memory lane.

Doug Larson

NOTHING

He that has done nothing has
known nothing.

Thomas Carlyle

I started out with nothing.
I still have most of it.

Michael Davis

In any moment of decision, the best thing
you can do is the right thing, the next
best thing is the wrong thing, and the worst
thing you can do is nothing.

OBEDIENCE

All who know well how to obey will know
also how to rule.

Flavius Josephus

OBLIGATION

When some men discharge an obligation you
can hear the report for miles around.

Mark Twain

OBSTACLES

If you find a path with no obstacles, it probably
doesn't lead anywhere.

Frank A. Clark

OLD AGE

Don't resent growing old. A great many
are denied the privilege.

He's so old his blood type was discontinued.

Bill Dana

I'm not saying he's old, but his birthday cake has just been declared a fire hazard.

How do you know when you're old? When you double your current age and realize you're not going to live that long.

Michael J. Leyden II

Old age does not announce itself.

Old age and sickness bring out the essential characteristics of a man.

Felix Frankfurter

In youth we run into difficulties, in old age difficulties run into us.

Josh Billings

OLD FASHIONS

Every generation laughs at the old fashions, but follows religiously the new.

Henry David Thoreau

ONCE

Once is the beginning of all things.

OPENNESS

Search me, O God, and know my heart: try me, and know my thoughts: and see if there be any wicked way in me.

Psalm 139:23

OPERA

Going to the opera, like getting drunk, is a sin that carries its own punishment with it, and that a very severe one.

Hannah Moore

Opera is when a guy gets stabbed in the back and instead of bleeding, he sings.

Ed Gardner

An unalterable and unquestioned law of the musical world required that the German text of French operas sung by Swedish artists should be translated into Italian for the clearer understanding of English-speaking audiences.

Edith Wharton

OPINION

We are so vain that we even care for the opinion of those we don't care for.

Marie von Ebner-Eschenbach

People do not seem to realize that their opinion of the world is also a confession of character.

Ralph Waldo Emerson

It were not best that we should all think alike; it is difference of opinion that makes the horse races.

Mark Twain

Do not think of knocking out another person's brains because he differs in opinion from you. It would be as rational to knock yourself on the head because you differ from yourself ten years ago.

Horace Mann

OPPORTUNITY

Small opportunities are often the beginning of great enterprises.

Demosthenes

We are all faced with a series of great opportunities brilliantly disguised as impossible situations.

Chuck Swindoll

Sometimes we stare so long at a door that is closing that we see too late the one that is open.

Alexander Graham Bell

I was seldom able to see an opportunity until it had ceased to be one.

Mark Twain

Watch out for emergencies. They are your big chance!

Fritz Reiner

Men do with opportunities as children do at the seashore: they fill their little hands with sand, and then let the grains fall through, one by one, till all are gone.

T. Jones

Too often, the opportunity knocks, but by the time you push back the chain, push back the bolt, unhook the two locks and shut off the burglar alarm, it's too late.

Rita Coolidge

It is often hard to distinguish between the hard knocks in life and those of opportunity.

Frederick Phillips

Americans want a good standard of living—not simply to accumulate possessions, but to fulfill a legitimate aspiration for an environment in which their families may live meaningful and happy lives. Our people are committed, therefore, to the creation and preservation of opportunity for every citizen, opportunity to lead a more rewarding life. They are equally committed to our alleviation of unavoidable misfortune and distress among their fellow citizens.

Dwight David Eisenhower

Next to knowing when to seize an opportunity, the most important thing in life is to know when to forego an advantage.

Benjamin Disraeli

Each problem has hidden in it an opportunity so powerful that it literally dwarfs the problem. The greatest success stories were created by people who recognized a problem and turned it into an opportunity.

Joseph Sugarman

OPPOSITION

Strong people are made by opposition, like kites that go up against the wind.

Frank Harris

You can measure a man by the opposition it takes to discourage him.

Robert C. Savage

OPTIMISM

Optimism: a cheerful frame of mind that enables a tea kettle to sing even though it's in hot water up to its nose.

ORIGINAL SIN

Original sin is in us, like the beard. We are shaved today and look clean, and have a smooth chin; tomorrow our beard has grown again. Nor does it cease growing while we remain on earth. In like manner original sin cannot be extirpated from us; it springs up in us as long as we live. Nevertheless we are bound to resist it to our utmost strength, and to cut it down unceasingly.

Martin Luther

OTHERS

People love others not for who they are but for how they make us feel!

Irwin Federman

OVERLOOK

People who overlook little slights and keep reaching out to help one another with acts of kindness will have very little problem maintaining harmonious relationships.

Richard Strauss

OVERWORK

Worry affects circulation, the heart and the glands, the whole nervous system and profoundly affects the heart. I have never known a man who died from overwork, but many who died from doubt.

Charles H. Mayo

PAIN

Pain nourishes courage. You can't be brave if you've only had wonderful things happen to you.

Mary Tyler Moore

Remember that pain has this most excellent quality: if prolonged, it cannot be severe, and if severe it cannot be prolonged.

Seneca

Pain is part of being alive, and we need to learn that. Pain does not last forever, nor is it necessarily unbearable, and we need to be taught that.

Harold Kushner

PARDON

Know all and you will pardon all.

Thomas à Kempis

Any man can seek revenge; it takes a king or prince to grant a pardon.

Arthur J. Rehrat

PASSION

What is man but his passion?

Robert Penn Warren

A strong passion for any object will ensure success, for the desire of the end will point out the means.

William Hazlitt

Be still when you have nothing to say; when genuine passion moves you, say what you've got to say, and say it hot.

D.H. Lawrence

The passions are the only orators which always persuade.

François de la Rochefoucauld

What a mistake to suppose that the passions are strongest in youth! The passions are not stronger, but the control over them is weaker! They are more easily excited, they are more violent and apparent; but they have less energy, less durability, less intense and concentrated power, than in maturer life.

Baron Lytton

Our passions are like convulsion fits, which, though they make us stronger for the time, leave us the weaker ever after.

Jonathan Swift

PAST

Old sins cast long shadows.

Your past is always going to be the way it was.
Stop trying to change it.

PATIENCE

Never think that God's delays are God's denials.
Hold on; hold fast; hold out. Patience is genius.

Georges Louis Leclerc de Buffon

There is no royal road to anything. One thing at a
time, and all things in succession. That which
grows slowly endures.

Josiah Gilbert Holland

Patience is the ability to wait until you're
too old to care anymore.

To know how to wait is the great secret
of success.

Joseph Marie de Maistre

Patience is a bitter plant, but it has sweet fruit.

The secret of patience is to do something
else in the meantime.

Have patience with all things, but chiefly have
patience with yourself. Do not lose courage in
considering your own imperfections, but instantly
set about remedying them—every day
begin the task anew.

Saint Francis de Sales

The very best and utmost of attainment in
this life is to remain still and let God act
and speak in thee.

Meister Eckhart

The string of one's sack of patience is
generally tied with a slipknot.

When you get into a tight place and everything
goes against you till it seems as though you
could not hold on a minute longer, never give
up then, for that is just the place and time that
the tide will turn.

Harriet Beecher Stowe

PATRIOTISM

Patriotism is easy to understand in America: it
means looking out for yourself by looking
out for your country.

Calvin Coolidge

Those who have not risen to the level of
patriotism are not likely to rise to higher levels.

Ralph Barton Perry

PEACE

Forgiving those who hurt us is the key
to personal peace.

G. Weatherley

Peace is not the absence of conflict, but the presence of God no matter what the conflict.

Peace of mind is that mental condition in which you have accepted the worst.

Lin Yutang

Five great enemies to peace inhabit with us: vice, avarice, ambition, envy, anger, and pride. If those enemies were to be banished, we should infallibly enjoy perpetual peace.

Petrarch

To be prepared for war is one of the most effectual means of preserving peace.

George Washington

The currency with which you pay for peace is made up of manly courage, fearless virility, readiness to serve justice and honor at any cost, and a mind and a heart attuned to sacrifice.

William Franklin Knox

For peace of mind, resign as general manager of the universe.

PEACEMAKERS

Blessed are the peacemakers: for they shall be called children of God.

Matthew 5:9

PENCIL

I am a little pencil in the hand of a writing God
who is sending a love letter to the world.

Mother Teresa

PEOPLE

People look at you and me to see what they are
supposed to be. And, if we don't disappoint them,
maybe, just maybe, they won't disappoint us.

Walt Disney

There are two kinds of people in the world: those
who walk into a room and say, "There you are,"
and those who say, "Here I am!"

Abigail Van Buren

Getting people to like you is merely the
other side of liking them.

Norman Vincent Peale

PERFECTION

He that will have a perfect brother must resign
himself to remaining brotherless.

PERFORMANCE

The finest eloquence is that which gets
things done.

David Lloyd George

Gentle in manner, strong in performance.

Claudio Aquaviva

PERPLEXITY

Trouble and perplexity drive me to prayer and prayer drives away perplexity and trouble.

Philip Melanchthen

PERSEVERANCE

The difference between perseverance and obstinacy is, that one often comes from a strong will, and the other from a strong won't.

Henry Ward Beecher

Keep on going, and the chances are that you will stumble on something, perhaps when you are least expecting it. I never heard of anyone ever stumbling on something sitting down.

Charles F. Kettering

PERSPECTIVE

All is perspective. To a worm, digging in the ground is more relaxing than going fishing.

Clyde Abel

PESSIMIST

The pessimist is the man who believes things couldn't possibly be worse, to which the optimist replies, "Oh yes they could."

Vladimir Bukovsky

No pessimist ever discovered the secrets of the stars, or sailed to an uncharted land, or opened a new heaven to the human spirit.

Helen Keller

PHILANTHROPY

Where there is the most love to God, there will be there the truest and most enlarged philanthropy.

Robert Southey

PICTURE

A picture is a poem without words.

Horace

A room hung with pictures, is a room hung with thoughts.

Sir Joshua Reynolds

PLAN

A life that hasn't a definite plan is likely to become driftwood.

David Sarnoff

PLANNING

Before you start looking for a peg, decide what hole you want to fill.

It is a mistake to look too far ahead. Only one link in the chain of destiny can be handled at a time.

Winston Churchill

PLAY

It is paradoxical that many educators and parents still differentiate between a time for learning and a time for play without seeing the vital connection between them.

Leo Buscaglia

You can discover more about a person in an hour of play than in a year of conversation.

Plato

PLEASE

You can please some of the people some of the time; you can please all of the people some of the time; but you can never please all the people all the time.

Abraham Lincoln

PLEASURE

The great source of pleasure is variety.

Samuel Johnson

One of the simple but genuine pleasures in life is getting up in the morning and hurrying to a mousetrap you set the night before.

Frank McKinney (Kin) Hubbard

The greatest pleasure I know is to do a good action by stealth and to have it found out by accident.

Charles Lamb

Tranquil pleasure lasts the longest; we are not fitted to bear the burden of great joy.

Christian Nestell Bovee

POETRY

You will not find poetry anywhere unless you bring some of it with you.

Joseph Joubert

POLITENESS

Politeness is the art of choosing among one's real thoughts.

Abel Stevens

Politeness is an inexpensive way of making friends.

William Feather

Politeness is not always the sign of wisdom, but the want of it always leave room for the suspicion of folly.

Walter Savage Landor

POLITICIANS

Bad officials are the ones elected by good citizens who do not vote.

George Jean Nathan

Here richly, with ridiculous display,
The politician's corpse was laid away.
While all of his acquaintance sneered and
slanged, I wept; for I had longed to
see him hanged.

Hilaire Belloc

Since a politician never believes what he says,
he is surprised when others believe him.

Charles DeGaulle

Ninety percent of the politicians give the
other ten percent a bad reputation.

Henry Kissinger

If a political candidate can't get up and make a
speech of his own, if he has to hire a press
agent to write it for him, then why not let the
press agent be the candidate?

Raymond Clapper

A politician is a man who shakes your
hand before election and your
confidence afterwards.

I know a politician who believes that there are
two sides to every question—and
takes them both.

Ken Murray

POLITICS

Political success is the ability, when the
inevitable occurs, to get credit for it.

Dr. Laurence J. Peter

The more you observe politics, the more you've got to admit that each party is worse than the other.

Will Rogers

Politics are almost as exciting as war, and quite dangerous. In war, you can only be killed once, but in politics many times.

Winston Churchill

The political parties that I would call great, are those which cling more to principles than to consequences; to general, and not to special cases; to ideas, and not to men. Such parties are usually distinguished by a nobler character, more generous passions, more genuine convictions, and a more bold and open conduct than others.

Alexis de Tocqueville

The fellow who stays home on election day because he doesn't want to have anything to do with crooked politics has a lot more to do with crooked politics than he thinks.

I looked up the word "politics" in the dictionary and it's actually a combination of two words: "poli," which means many, and "tics," which means bloodsuckers.

Jay Leno

POOR

There are two things needed in these days; first, for rich men to find out how poor men live; and second, for poor men to know how rich men work.

Edward Atkinson

Defend the poor and fatherless: do justice to
the afflicted and needy.

Psalm 82:3

There is one advantage of being poor—a doctor
will cure you faster.

Frank McKinney (Kin) Hubbard

POSITIVE THINKING

There is in the worst of fortune the best of
chances for a happy change.

Euripides

POTENTIAL

Our nation was founded as an experiment in
human liberty. Its institutions reflect the belief of
our founders that men had their origin and destiny
in God; that they were endowed by Him with
inalienable rights and had duties prescribed by
moral law, and that human institutions ought
primarily to help men develop their
God-given possibilities.

John Foster Dulles

POVERTY

Neither great poverty nor great riches
will hear reason.

Henry Fielding

We are not going to perpetuate poverty by substituting a permanent dole for a pay check. There is no humanity or charity in destroying self reliance, dignity, and self respect . . . the very substance of moral fiber. We seek reforms that will, wherever possible, change relief check to pay check.

Ronald Reagan

POWER

Temptations which accompany the working day will be conquered on the basis of the morning breakthrough to God. Decisions, demanded by work, become easier and simpler where they are made not in the fear of men, but only in the sight of God. He wants to give us today the power which we need for our work.

Dietrich Bonhoeffer

Nearly all men can stand adversity, but if you want to test a man's character, give him power.

Abraham Lincoln

Being powerful is like being a lady: If you have to tell people you are, you aren't.

Margaret Thatcher

PRACTICAL

You cannot sell the cow and sup the milk.

Don't sell the skin till you have caught the bear.

PRAISE

Make a joyful noise unto the LORD.

Psalm 100:1

Praise teachers while they are present,
subordinates when their work is done,
and friends when absent.

Get someone else to blow your horn and the
sound will carry twice as far.

Will Rogers

Try praising your wife, even if it does
frighten her at first.

Billy Sunday

Finally, brethren, whatsoever things are true,
whatsoever things are honest, whatsoever things
are just, whatsoever things are pure, whatsoever
things are lovely, whatsoever things are of good
report; if there be any virtue, and if there be
any praise, think on these things.

Philippians 4:8

PRAYER

If you can't pray as you want to, pray as
you can. God knows what you mean.

Vance Havner

Every time we pray our horizon is altered, our
attitude to things is altered, not sometimes
but every time, and the amazing thing is that
we don't pray more.

Oswald Chambers

When you pray for anyone you tend to modify
your personal attitude toward him.

Norman Vincent Peale

But thou, when thou prayest, enter into thy closet,
and when thou has shut thy door, pray to thy
father which is in secret; and thy Father which
seeth in secret shall reward thee openly.

Matthew 6:6

Do not pray for easy lives, pray to be stronger
men. Do not pray for tasks equal to your powers,
pray for powers equal to your tasks.

Phillips Brooks

The less I pray, the harder it gets; the more I pray,
the better it goes.

Martin Luther

Confess your faults one to another, and pray one
for another, that ye may be healed. The effectual
fervent prayer of a righteous man availeth much.

James 5:16

Teach us to pray that we may cause
The enemy to flee,
That we his evil power may bind,
His prisoners to free.

Watchman Nee

Don't force your child to pray. Instead, every night set aside fifteen minutes before his bedtime for reading and conversation. Show him pictures of Jesus, and tell him stories of the Savior. Talk to him of the Heavenly Father. Explain to him that God sends the sun and rain. Tell him it is God who makes the flowers grow, and gives us food to eat. Then lead him in prayers of thanksgiving and prayers asking the Heavenly Father for guidance and protection.

Billy Graham

Prayer at its best is the expression of the total life for, all things else being equal, our prayers are only as powerful as our lives.

A.W. Tozer

A problem not worth praying about is not worth worrying about.

There are four ways God answers prayer: no, not yet; no, I love you too much; yes, I thought you'd never ask; yes, and here's more.

Anne Lewis

The potency of prayer hath subdued the strength of fire; it hath bridled the rage of lions, hushed anarchy to rest, extinguished wars, appeased the elements, expelled demons, burst the chains of death, expanded the gates of heaven, assuaged diseases, repelled frauds, rescued cities from destruction, stayed the sun in its course, and arrested the progress of the thunderbolt.

Saint John Chrysostom

Dealing in generalities is the death of prayer.

J.H. Evans

In seasons of distress and grief,
My soul has often found relief,
And oft escaped the tempter's snare,
By thy return, sweet hour of prayer.

W.W. Walford

All who call on God in true faith, earnestly from
the heart, will certainly be heard, and will receive
what they have asked and desired.

Martin Luther

By prayer we couple the powers of heaven to our
helplessness, the powers which can capture
strongholds and make the impossible possible.

O. Hallesby

Faith, and hope, and patience, and all the strong,
beautiful, vital forces of piety are withered and
dead in a prayerless life. The life of the individual
believer, his personal salvation, and personal
Christian graces have their being, bloom, and
fruitage in prayer.

E.M. Bounds

Seven days without prayer makes one weak.

Allen E. Bartlett

There come times when I have nothing more to
tell God. If I were to continue to pray in words, I
would have to repeat what I have already said. At
such times it is wonderful to say to God, "May I be
in Thy presence, Lord? I have nothing more to say
to Thee, but I do love to be in Thy presence."

O. Hallesby

We can do nothing without prayer. All things can be done by importunate prayer. It surmounts or removes all obstacles, overcomes every resisting force, and gains its ends in the face of invincible hindrances.

E.M. Bounds

Prayer does not change God, but it changes him who prays.

Soren Kierkegaard

Restraining prayer, we cease to fight;
Prayer keeps the Christian's armor bright;
And Satan trembles when he sees
The weakest saint upon his knees.

William Cowper

See to it, night and day, that you pray for your children. Then you will leave them a great legacy of answers to prayer, which will follow them all the days of their life. Then you may calmly and with a good conscience depart from them, even though you may not leave them a great deal of material wealth.

O. Hallesby

Prayer is the great engine to overthrow and rout my spiritual enemies, the great means to procure the graces of which I stand in hourly need.

John Newton

When at night you cannot sleep, talk to the Shepherd and stop counting sheep.

Unless I had the spirit of prayer, I could do nothing.

Charles G. Finney

We look upon prayer as a means of getting things for ourselves; the Bible's idea of prayer is that we may get to know God Himself.

Oswald Chambers

The value of consistent prayer is not that He will hear us, but that we will hear Him.

William McGill

The purpose of prayer is to reveal the presence of God equally present, all the time, in every condition.

Oswald Chambers

No one is a firmer believer in the power of prayer than the devil; not that he practices it, but he suffers from it.

Guy H. King

God shapes the world by prayer. Prayers are deathless. They outlive the lives of those who uttered them.

E.M. Bounds

I have been driven many times to my knees by the overwhelming conviction that I had nowhere else to go. My own wisdom and that of all about me seemed insufficient for the day.

Abraham Lincoln

Though we cannot by our prayers give God any information, yet we must by our prayers give him honor.

Matthew Henry

Praying which does not result in pure conduct is a delusion. We have missed the whole office and virtue of praying if it does not rectify conduct. It is in the very nature of things that we must quit praying, or quit bad conduct.

E.M. Bounds

PSYCHOBABBLE

To err is dysfunctional, to forgive co-dependent.

Berton Averre

Neurotic means he is not as sensible as I am, and psychotic means he's even worse than my brother-in-law.

Karl Menninger

PUBLIC FIGURE

He that puts on a public gown, must put off a private person.

PUBLICITY

What kills a skunk is the publicity it gives itself.

Abraham Lincoln

PURE

When men are pure, laws are useless; when men are corrupt, laws are broken.

Benjamin Disraeli

PURPOSE

My research offers impressive evidence that we feel better when we attempt to make our world better . . . to have a purpose beyond one's self lends to existence a meaning and direction—the most important characteristic of high well-being.

Gail Sheehy

More men fail through lack of purpose than through lack of talent.

Billy Sunday

True happiness . . . is not attained through self-gratification, but through fidelity to a worthy purpose.

Helen Keller

If a man hasn't discovered something that he will die for, he isn't fit to live.

Martin Luther King Jr.

When you buy a vase cheap, look for the flaw; when someone offers favors, search for their purpose.

Great minds have purposes; others have wishes. Little minds are tamed and subdued by misfortune, but great minds rise above them.

Washington Irving

PREACHING

When I hear a man preach, I like to see him act as if he were fighting bees.

Abraham Lincoln

I preached as never sure to preach again, and as a dying man to dying men.

Richard Baxter

PREJUDICES

Everyone is a prisoner of his own experiences. No one can eliminate prejudices—just recognize them.

Edward R. Murrow

PRESENT

If there is hope in the future, there is power in the present.

John Maxwell

I don't think we understand the importance of the present; there's nothing more important than what you are doing now.

Harold Clurman

PRESENTATION

A person will accept or reject your proposal in the first nine minutes of your presentation.

PRESIDENT

I know that when things don't go well, they like to blame the president, and that is one of the things presidents are paid for.

John F. Kennedy

No man will ever bring out of the presidency the reputation which carries him into it.

Thomas Jefferson

PRIDE

As Plato entertained some friends in a room where there was a couch richly ornamented, Diogenes came in very dirty, as usual, and getting upon the couch, and trampling on it, said, "I trample upon the pride of Plato." Plato mildly answered, "But with greater pride, Diogenes!"

Desderius Erasmus

It was pride that changed angels into devils; it is humility that makes men as angels.

Augustine of Hippo

He who lives only to benefit himself confers on the world a benefit when he dies.

Tertullian

God resisteth the proud, and giveth grace to the humble.

1 Peter 5:5

PRINCIPLE

In vain do they talk of happiness who never subdued an impulse in obedience to a principle. He who never sacrificed a present to a future good, or a personal to a general one, can speak of happiness only as the blind do of colors.

Horace Mann

It is easier to fight for one's principles than to live up to them.

Alfred Adler

PROBLEMS

Every problem has in it the seeds of its own solution. If you don't have any problems, you don't get any seeds.

Norman Vincent Peale

Everybody has a problem, is a problem, or has to live with a problem.

Sam Shoemaker

A man with fifty problems is twice as alive as a man with twenty-five. If you haven't got problems, you should get down on your knees and ask "Lord, don't you trust me anymore?"

John Bainbridge

The greatest and most important problems in life are all in a certain sense insoluble. They can never be solved, but only outgrown.

Carl Jung

God brings men into deep waters not to drown them, but to cleanse them.

Aughey

The significant problems we face cannot be solved at the same level of thinking we were at when we created them.

Albert Einstein

PROCRASTINATION

It is an undoubted truth that the less one has to do the less time one finds to do it in. One yawns, one procrastinates, one can do it when one will, and therefore, one seldom does it at all; whereas, those who have a great deal of business must buckle to it; and then they always find time enough to do it.

Philip Dormer Stanhope

Putting off an easy thing makes it hard, and putting off a hard one makes it impossible.

George Horace Lorimer

He that rises late must trot all day.

PROFESSOR

A professor is one who talks in someone else's sleep.

W.H. Auden

There was an old cannibal whose stomach suffered from so many disorders that he could only digest animals that had no spines. Thus, for years, he subsisted only upon university professors.

Louis Phillips

PROGRESS

The art of progress is to preserve order amid change, and to preserve change amid order. Life refuses to be embalmed alive.

Alfred North Whitehead

Progress is the real cure for an
over-estimate of ourselves.

George Macdonald

PROMISE

Politicians and roosters crow about what
they intend to do. The roosters deliver
what is promised.

He who is most slow in making a promise
is the most faithful in its performance.

Jean Jacques Rousseau

When a man repeats a promise again and
again, he means to fail you.

Edmund Fuller

Magnificent promises are always
to be suspected.

Theodore Parker

PROSPEROUS

The reason American cities are prosperous is
that there is no place to sit down.

Alfred Joseph Talley

PROTESTANTISM

The true force of Protestantism was its signal
return to the individual conscience—to the
method of Jesus.

Matthew Arnold

PRIDE

When a proud man hears another praised,
he feels himself injured.

None are more taken in by flattery than the proud,
who wish to be the first and are not.

Baruch Spinoza

QUICKLY

Good and quickly seldom meet.

QUOTATIONS

He wrapped himself in quotations as a
beggar would enfold himself in the
purple of emperors.

Rudyard Kipling

RAGE

People who fly into a rage always
make a bad landing.

Will Rogers

RANK

It is an interesting question how far
men would retain their relative rank if
they were divested of their clothes.

Henry David Thoreau

READING

Reading Christians are growing Christians.
When Christians cease to read,
they cease to grow.

John Wesley

When we read too fast or too slowly,
we understand nothing.

Blaise Pascal

REALISTIC DECISION

If someone tells you he is going to make a "realistic decision," you immediately understand that he has resolved to do something bad.

Mary McCarthy

REALITY

A body shouldn't heed what might be. He's got to do with what is.

Louis L'Amour

REASON

St. Augustine teaches that there is in each man a Serpent, an Eve, and an Adam. Our senses and natural propensities are the Serpent; the excitable desire is Eve; and the reason is the Adam. Our nature tempts us perpetually; criminal desire is often excited; but sin is not completed till reason consents.

Blaise Pascal

REFORM

Nothing so needs reforming as other people's habits.

Mark Twain

REGRET

Regret is an appalling waste of energy: you can't build on it; it's only good for wallowing in.

Katherine Mansfield

RELATIVITY

When a man sits with a pretty girl for an hour, it
seems like a minute. But let him sit on a hot stove
for a minute, and it's longer than any hour.
That's relativity.

Albert Einstein

RELIEF

For fast-acting relief try slowing down.

Lily Tomlin

RELIGION

Most people have some sort of religion.
At least they know which church they're
staying away from.

John Erskine

Some would divorce morality from religion;
but religion is the root without which
morality would die.

Cyrus Augustus Bartol

RELIGIOUS LIBERTY

The love of religious liberty is a stronger sentiment, when fully excited, than an attachment to civil freedom. Conscience, in the cause of religion, prepares the mind to act and to suffer beyond almost all other causes. It sometimes gives an impulse so irresistible that no fetters of power or of opinion can withstand it. History instructs us that this love of religious liberty, made up of the clearest sense of right and the highest conviction of duty, is able to look the sternest despotism in the face, and, with means apparently inadequate, to shake principalities and powers.

Daniel Webster

RELUCTANCE

There is a strange reluctance on the part of most people to admit that they enjoy life.

William Lyon Phelps

REMEDIES

He that will not apply new remedies must expect new evils.

Francis Bacon

Our remedies oft in ourselves do lie.

William Shakespeare

REMORSE

Remorse begets reform.

William Cowper

RENEW

Inside myself is a place where I live all alone,
and that's where you renew your springs
that never dry up.

Pearl Buck

REPARTEE

Repartee is a duel fought with the
points of jokes.

Max Forrester Eastman

REPENTANCE

True repentance is to cease from sinning.

Ambrose of Milan

Repentance is a hearty sorrow for our past
misdeeds, and is a sincere resolution and
endeavor, to the utmost of our power, to conform
all our actions to the law of God. It does not
consist in one single act of sorrow, but in doing
works meet for repentance; in a sincere
obedience to the law of Christ for the
remainder of our lives.

John Locke

REPOSE

All mankind's unhappiness derives from
one thing: his inability to know how to
remain in repose in one room.

Blaise Pascal

REPUTATION

Those who are once found to be bad are presumed so forever.

A reputation once broken may possibly be repaired, but the world will always keep their eyes on the spot where the crack was.

Joseph Hall

Much of reputation depends on the period in which it rises. In dark periods, when talents appear, they shine like the sun through a small hole in the window-shutter, and the strong beam dazzles amid the surrounding gloom. Open the shutter, and the general diffusion of light attracts no notice.

Sir Robert Walpole

A wounded reputation is seldom cured.

Don't talk about yourself; it will be done when you leave.

Addison Mitzner

Do you wish men to speak well of you? Then never speak well of yourself.

Blaise Pascal

RESPECT

All objects lose by too familiar a view.

John Dryden

RESPONSIBILITY

Responsibility is the thing people dread
most of all. Yet it is the one thing in the world that
develops us, gives us manhood or
womanhood fibre.

Frank Crane

No man will succeed unless he is ready to face
and overcome difficulties, and is prepared
to assume responsibilities.

William J.H. Boetcher

Unto whomsoever much is given, of him
shall be much required.

Luke 12:48

A new position of responsibility will usually
show a man to be a far stronger creature
than was supposed.

William James

REST

Unless we come apart and rest a while,
we may just plain come apart.

Vance Havner

RESTLESSNESS

Restlessness is discontent, and discontent is the
first necessity of progress. Show me a thoroughly
satisfied man and I will show you a failure.

Thomas Alva Edison

RESTROOM

Mark my words, when a society has to
resort to the restroom for its humor, the writing
is on the wall.

Alan Bennett

RESULTS

Unstringing the bow does not cure the wound.

RETIREMENT

The best time to start thinking about
your retirement is before the boss does.

A man is known by the company that keeps
him on after retirement age.

REVENGE

To refrain from imitation is the best revenge.

Marcus Aurelius

The best manner of avenging ourselves is by not
resembling him who has injured us.

Jane Porter

RHETORIC

The best rules of rhetoric are to speak
intelligently; speak from the heart; have
something to say, say it; and stop when
you're done.

Tryon Edwards

RICH

You can't spend yourself rich any more
than you can drink yourself sober.

Herman E. Talmadge

Few things have been more productive of
controversy over the ages than the suggestion
that the rich should, by one device or another,
share their wealth with those who are not.

John Kenneth Galbraith

Don't knock the rich. When did a poor
person give you a job?

Dr. Laurence J. Peter

RIDICULE

Ridicule is the weapon most feared by enthusiasts
of every description; from its predominance over
such minds it often checks what is absurd, but
fully as often smothers that which is noble.

Sir Walter Scott

RIGHT

Nothing which is morally wrong can ever
be politically right.

It's an odd thing about this universe that, though
we all disagree with each other, we are all of us
always in the right.

Logan Pearsall Smith

Right wrongs no man.

Do right and fear no man.

RIGHT TRACK

Even if you're on the right track, you'll get
run over if you just sit there.

Will Rogers

RISK

In order to find the edge, you must risk
going over the edge.

Dennis Dugan

No man is worth his salt who is not ready
at all times to risk his well-being, to risk
his body, to risk his life, in a great cause.

Theodore Roosevelt

Everything is sweetened by risk.

Alexander Smith

Only those who will risk going too far can
possibly find out how far one can go.

T.S. Eliot

Yes, risk-taking is inherently failure-prone.
Otherwise, it would be
called sure-thing-taking.

Tim McMahon

Unless you enter the tiger's den,
you cannot take the cubs.

By exposing yourself to risk, you're exposing yourself to heavy-duty learning, which gets you on all levels. It becomes a very emotional experience as well as an intellectual experience. Each time you make a mistake, you're learning from the school of hard knocks, which is the best education available.

Gifford Pinchot

Behold the turtle. He makes progress only when he sticks his neck out.

James Bryant Conant

Great deeds are usually wrought at great risks.

Herodotus

ROBBERY

I thank Thee first because I was never robbed before; second because although they took my purse they did not take my life; third, because although they took my all, it was not much; and fourth because it was I who was robbed, and not I who robbed.

Matthew Henry

ROMANCES

As soon as histories are properly told there is no more need of romances.

Walt Whitman

ROUGH

I grew up in a neighborhood so rough,
I learned to read by the light of
a police helicopter.

Bill Jones

RUIN

All men that are ruined are ruined on
the side of their natural propensities.

Edmund Burke

SAFETY

Nothing will ruin the country if the people themselves will undertake its safety; and nothing can save it if they leave that safety in any hands but their own.

Daniel Webster

SALESMEN

Salesmen who wear out their pants before their shoes are making contact in the wrong places.

SATISFACTION

The amount of satisfaction you get from life depends largely on your own ingenuity, self-sufficiency, and resourcefulness. People who wait around for life to supply their satisfaction usually find boredom instead.

William Menninger

SCANDAL

Scandal dies sooner of itself,
than we could kill it.

Benjamin Rush

SCRIPTURE

Nobody ever outgrows Scripture; the book
widens and deepens with our years.

Charles Haddon Spurgeon

All scripture is given by inspiration of God,
and is profitable for doctrine, for reproof,
for correction, for instruction in righteousness:
That the man of God may be perfect,
throughly furnished unto all good works.

2 Timothy 3:16,17

Search the scriptures; for in them ye think
ye have eternal life; and they are they
which testify of me.

John 5:39

SCULPTOR

You show me a sculptor who works in
the basement and I'll show you a
low-down chiseler!

Soupy Sales

SECRET

Three may keep a secret if two of
them are dead.

Benjamin Franklin

To know that one has a secret is to
know half the secret itself.

Henry Ward Beecher

To keep your secret is wisdom; but to expect
others to keep it is folly.

Oliver Wendell Holmes

Nothing is so burdensome as a secret.

Secrets are things we give to others
to keep for us.

Elbert Hubbard

SECURITY

If you want total security, go to prison.
There you're fed, clothed, given medical
care, and so on. The only thing
lacking . . . is freedom.

Dwight D. Eisenhower

Security is not the absence of danger,
but the presence of God, no matter
what the danger.

We spend our time searching for security
and hate it when we get it.

John Steinbeck

Security is mostly a superstition. It does not exist in nature, nor do the children of men as a whole experience it. Avoiding danger is no safer in the long run than outright exposure. Life is either a daring adventure, or nothing. Serious harm, I am afraid, has been wrought to our generation by fostering the idea that they would live secure in a permanent order of things. They have expected stability and find none within themselves or in their universe. Before it is too late they must learn and teach others that only by brave acceptance of change and all-time crisis-ethics can they rise to the height of superlative responsibility.

Helen Keller

SELF-CONTROL

What a curious phenomenon it is that you can get men to die for the liberty of the world who will not make the little sacrifice that is needed to free themselves from their own individual bondage.

Bruce Barton

The best time for you to hold your tongue is the time you feel you must say something or bust.

Josh Billings

SELF-DENIAL

Men who have attained things worth having in
this world have worked while others idled, have
persevered when others gave up in despair, have
practiced early in life the valuable habits of
self-denial, industry, and singleness of purpose.
As a result, they enjoy in later life the success
so often erroneously attributed to good luck.

Grenville Kleiser

SELF-DISCIPLINE

He who conquers others is strong; he who
conquers himself is mighty.

Lao-tzu

No steam or gas ever drives anything until it is
confined. No Niagara is ever turned into light and
power until it is tunneled. No life ever grows until
it is focused, dedicated, disciplined.

Harry Emerson Fosdick

He that hath no rule over his own spirit is like a
city that is broken down, and without walls.

Proverbs 25:28

What we do upon some great occasion will
probably depend on what we already are; and
what we are will be the result of previous
years of self-discipline.

Henry Parry Liddon

SELF-EVALUATION

If you don't like something about yourself,
change it. If you can't change it, accept it.

Ted Shackelford

It is doubtless a vice to turn one's eyes
inward too much, but I am my own
comedy and tragedy.

Ralph Waldo Emerson

SELF-EXAMINATION

Sometimes it is more important to
discover what one cannot do,
than what one can do.

Lin Yutang

The life which is unexamined is
not worth living.

Plato

As we advance in life, we learn the
limits of our abilities.

J.A. Froud

SELFISHNESS

Selfishness is the root and source
of all natural and moral evils.

Nathaniel Emmons

If you wish to be miserable, think about yourself; about what you want, what you like, what respect people ought to pay you, what people think of you; and then to you nothing will be pure. You will spoil everything you touch; you will make sin and misery for yourself out of everything God sends you; you will be as wretched as you choose.

Charles Kingsley

SELF-KNOWLEDGE

A humble knowledge of oneself is a surer road to God than a deep searching of the sciences.

Thomas à Kempis

SELF-RESPECT

Self-respect cannot be hunted. It cannot be purchased. It is never for sale. It cannot be fabricated out of public relations. It comes to us when we are alone, in quiet moments, in quiet places, when we suddenly realize that, knowing the good, we have done it; knowing the beautiful, we have served it; knowing the truth, we have spoken it.

Alfred Whitney Griswold

SELF-SACRIFICE

For anything worth having one must pay the price; and the price is always work, patience, love, self-sacrifice—no paper currency, no promises to pay, but the gold of real service.

John Burroughs

SENATE

Ancient Rome declined because it had a Senate; now what's going to happen to us with both a Senate and a House?

Will Rogers

SERMON

Few sinners are saved after the first twenty minutes of a sermon.

Mark Twain

It is easier to go six miles to hear a sermon, than to spend one quarter of an hour in meditating on it when I come home.

Philip Henry

SERVE

One thing I know: the only ones among you who will be really happy are those who will have sought and found how to serve.

Albert Schweitzer

The high destiny of the individual is to serve rather than to rule.

Albert Einstein

Men are especially intolerant of serving, and being ruled by, their equals.

Baruch Spinoza

SEVEN AGES OF MAN

The seven ages of man: spills, drills,
thrills, bills, ills, pills, wills.

Richard J. Needham

SEVEN SINS

The seven sins are wealth without works,
pleasure without conscience, knowledge
without character, commerce without morality,
science without humanity, worship without
sacrifice, and politics without principle.

Mahatma Gandhi

SHIP

The man who has done nothing but wait
for his ship to come in has already
missed the boat.

SHOES

I did not have three thousand pairs of shoes,
I had one thousand and sixty.

Imelda Marcos

SHOPPING

A place where a woman goes when
she's got nothing to wear.

SHORT SERMON

The world's shortest sermon:
"When in doubt, don't."

SHORTSIGHTED

One never notices what has been done; one can only see what remains to be done . . .

Marie Curie

SILENCE

Silence is not always golden—sometimes it's guilt.

Silence is one great art of conversation.

William Hazlitt

SIMPLE

All the great things are simple, and many can be expressed in a single word: freedom; justice; honor; duty; mercy; hope.

Sir Winston Churchill

SIN

The recognition of sin is the beginning of salvation.

Martin Luther

One leak will sink a ship, and one sin will destroy a sinner.

John Bunyan

Sin is first pleasing, then it grows easy, then delightful, then frequent, then habitual, then confirmed; then the man is impenitent, then he is obstinate, then he is resolved never to repent, and then he is ruined.

Robert Leighton

SIXTY-FIVE

My, my—65! I guess this marks the first
day of the rest of our life savings.

H. Martin

SLANDER

No one is safe from slander. The best
way is to pay no attention to it, but live in
innocence and let the world talk.

Molière

The slanderer and the assassin differ only in the
weapon they use; with the one it is the dagger,
with the other the tongue. The former is worse
than the latter, for the last only kills the body, while
the other murders the reputation and peace.

Tryon Edwards

Believe nothing against another, but on good
authority; nor report what may hurt another,
unless it be a greater hurt to some
other to conceal it.

William Penn

Next to the slanderer, we detest the
bearer of the slander to our ears.

Mary Catherwood

To speak ill of others is a dishonest way of
praising ourselves; let us be above such
transparent egotism . . . If you can't say good and
encouraging things, say nothing. Nothing is
often a good thing to say, and always a
clever thing to say.

Will Durant

Character assassination is at once easier and surer than physical assault; and it involves far less risk for the assassin. It leaves him free to commit the same deed over and over again, and may, indeed, win him the honors of a hero even in the country of his victims.

Alan Barth

SLANG

Slang is a language that rolls up its sleeves, spits on its hands and goes to work.

Carl Sandburg

SLAVERY

From my earliest youth I have regarded slavery as a great moral and political evil. I think it unjust, repugnant to the natural equality of mankind, founded only in superior power; a standing and permanent conquest by the stronger over the weaker. The religion of Christ is a religion of kindness, justice, and brotherly love: but slavery is not kindly affectionate; it does not seek another's and not its own; it does not let the oppressed go free; it is but a continual act of oppression.

Daniel Webster

SLEEP

What the will and reason are powerless to remove, sleep melts like snow in water.

Walter John de la Mare

SMALL DELIGHTS

A multitude of small delights constitute happiness.

Charles Baudelaire

SMELL

Offensive-smelling people do not notice their own smell.

SMILE

A smile is an inexpensive way to improve your looks.

Charles Gordy

A smile is the whisper of a laugh.

Wear a smile and have friends; wear a scowl and have wrinkles.

George Eliot

A smile is a light on your face to let someone know you are at home.

No matter how grouchy you're feeling,
You'll find the smile more or less healing.
It grows in a wreath
All around the front teeth—
Thus preserving the face from congealing.

Anthony Euwer

A smile is a powerful weapon; you
can even break ice with it.

SMOKING

Smoking is one of the leading causes
of statistics.

Fletcher Knebel

I started smoking to lose weight. After I
dropped that lung I felt pretty good.

Michael Meehan

SNEER

Who can refute a sneer? It is independent
of proof, reason, argument, or sense, and
may as well be used against facts and truth,
as against falsehood.

Charles Simmons

SNIFFLES

Life is made up of sobs, sniffles, and smiles,
with sniffles predominating.

O. Henry

SNOOPING

Those who pry into other people's affairs will
hear what they do not like.

Libyan

SNORE

Laugh and the world laughs with you;
snore and you sleep alone.

Anthony Burgess

SOAP OPERAS

I worry that our lives are like soap operas. We can
go for months and not tune in to them, then six
months later we look in and the same stuff is
still going on.

Jane Wagner

SOCIETY

What can you say about a society that says God
is dead and Elvis is alive?

Irv Kupcinet

To get into the best society nowadays, one
has either to feed people, amuse people,
or shock people.

Oscar Wilde

SONG

A song will outlive all sermons in the memory.

Henry Giles

SORROW

We have no right to ask when a sorrow comes,
"Why did this happen to me?" unless we ask the
same question for every joy that comes our way.

Philip E. Bernstein

He that increaseth knowledge
increaseth sorrow.

Ecclesiastes 1:18

Sorrow will pay no debt.

Any person who is always feeling sorry
for himself, should be.

Sorrow is like a precious treasure, shown
only to friends.

There is something pleasurable in calm
remembrance of a past sorrow.

Cicero

One can endure sorrow alone, but it takes
two to be glad.

Elbert Hubbard

Have courage for the great sorrows of life and
patience for the small ones. And when you have
finished your daily task, go to sleep in peace.
God is awake.

Victor Hugo

SOUL

Money is not required to buy one
necessity of the soul.

Henry David Thoreau

SPEECH

Not only to say the right thing in the right place, but far more difficult, to leave unsaid the wrong thing at the tempting moment.

George Sala

Never hold anyone by the button or the hand in order to be heard out; for if people are unwilling to hear you, you had better hold your tongue than them.

Lord Chesterfield

Blessed is the man who, having nothing to say, abstains from giving wordy evidence of the fact.

George Eliot

SPEED

I've always found that the speed of the boss is the speed of the team.

Lee Iacocca

SPIRIT

There are only two forces in the world, the sword and the spirit. In the long run the sword will always be conquered by the spirit.

Napoleon Bonaparte

STAGE OF LIFE

Every stage of life has its troubles, and no man is content with his own age.

Ausonius

STAR

I always thought I should be treated like a star.

Madonna

STARTING

Well begun is half done.

STICKY

Even when freshly washed and relieved of all obvious confections, children tend to be sticky.

Fran Lebowitz

STRANGERS

If a man be gracious to strangers, it shows that he is a citizen of the world, and his heart is no island, cut off from other islands, but a continent that joins them.

Francis Bacon

STRENGTH

Don't hit at all if it is honorably possible to avoid hitting, but never hit soft.

Theodore Roosevelt

Don't expect to build up the weak by pulling down the strong.

Calvin Collidge

STRESS

Don't be too afraid to enjoy the stress of a full life nor too naïve to think you can do so without some intelligent thinking and planning. Man should not try to avoid stress any more than he would shun food, love, or exercise.

Hans Selye

Most stress is caused by people who overestimate the importance of their problems.

Michael LeBoeuf

Times of stress and difficulty are seasons of opportunity when the seeds of progress are sown.

Thomas F. Woodlock

STRIFE

The law of worthy life is fundamentally the law of strife; it is only through labor and painful effort, by grim energy and resolute courage that we move into better things.

Theodore Roosevelt

STRIVE

I have always found that to strive with a superior, is injurious; with an equal, doubtful; with an inferior, sordid and base; with any, full of unquietness.

Joseph Hall

STRUGGLE

The struggle alone pleases us, not
the victory.

Blaise Pascal

STUDY

If you devote your time to study, you will avoid all
the irksomeness of this life, nor will you long for
the approach of night, being tired of the day; nor
will you be a burden to yourself, nor your society
insupportable to others.

Seneca

STUPID

This man Wellington is so stupid he does not
know when he is beaten, and goes on fighting.

Napoleon Bonaparte

SUCCESS

Flaming enthusiasm, backed up by horse
sense and persistence, is the quality that most
frequently makes for success.

Dale Carnegie

The secret of my success is that at an early age I
discovered I was not God.

Oliver Wendell Holmes Jr.

One of the biggest factors in success is the
courage to undertake something.

James A. Worsham

God may allow His servant to succeed when He has disciplined him to a point where he does not need to succeed to be happy. The man who is elated by success and is a cast down by failure is still a carnal man. At best his fruit will have a worm in it.

A.W. Tozer

Success seems to be largely a matter of hanging on after others have let go.

William Feather

Success is to be measured not so much by the position that one has reached in life as by the obstacles which he has overcome.

Booker T. Washington

The most important single ingredient in the formula of success is knowing how to get along with people.

Theodore Roosevelt

All you need in this life is ignorance and confidence; then success is sure.

Mark Twain

The gent who wakes up and finds himself a success hasn't been asleep.

Wilson Mizner

If you want a place in the sun, you've got to put up with a few blisters.

Abigail Van Buren

I hope someday to have so much of what the world calls success, that people will ask me, "What's your secret?" and I will tell them, "I just get up again when I fall down."

Paul Harvey

If you wish success in life, make perseverance your bosom friend, experience your wise counselor, caution your elder brother, and hope your guardian genius.

Joseph Addison

Man can climb to the highest summits but cannot dwell there long.

George Bernard Shaw

I was successful because you believed in me.

Ulysses S. Grant

SUFFERING

What really raises one's indignation against suffering is not suffering intrinsically, but the senselessness of suffering.

Friedrich Wilhelm Nietzsche

Although the world is full of suffering, it is full also of the overcoming of it.

Helen Keller

Pain is inevitable. Suffering is optional.

The chief pang of most trials is not so much the actual suffering itself as our own spirit of resistance to it.

Jean Nicholas Grou

We are healed of a suffering only by experiencing it to the full.

Marcel Proust

I have often noticed that the suffering which is most difficult, if not impossible, to forgive is unreal, imagined suffering . . . The worst, most obstinate grievances are imagined ones.

Laurens van der Post

SUICIDE

Suicide is 180 degree murder.

R. E. Phillips

SURPRISED

When I was born I was so surprised I didn't talk for a year and a half.

Gracie Allen

SUSPICION

Suspicion is the poison of true friendship.

Augustine of Hippo

SWEARING

He that will swear, will lie.

The foolish and wicked practice of profane cursing
and swearing is a vice so mean and low that
every person of sense and character detests
and despises it.

George Washington

It chills my blood to hear the blest Supreme
rudely appealed to on each trifling theme.
Maintain your rank, vulgarity despise.
To swear is neither brave, polite,
nor wise.

William Cowper

TACT

Tact consists in knowing how far
we may go too far.

Jean Cocteau

TALK

Remember, every time you open your
mouth to talk, your mind walks out and
parades up and down the words.

Edwin H. Stuart

There are few wild beasts more to be dreaded
than a talking man having nothing to say.

Jonathan Swift

It is good speaking that improves good silence.

Talk low, talk slow, and don't say too much.

John Wayne

TALK SHOW

In the Soviet Union a writer who is critical, as we
know, is taken to a lunatic asylum. In the United
States, he's taken to a talk show.

Carlos Fuentes

TASKS

Attempt easy tasks as if they were difficult, and difficult as if they were easy; in the one case that confidence may not fall asleep, in the other that it may not be dismayed.

Baltasar Gracian

I long to accomplish a great and noble task, but it's my chief duty to accomplish small tasks as if they were great and noble.

Helen Keller

TAX COLLECTOR

The tax collector must love poor people—he's creating so many of them.

Bill Vaughan

TEACHING

Teach the small and the lowly gently; the needle with a small eye should be threaded slowly.

Good teaching is one-fourth preparation and three-fourths theater.

Gail Godwin

TEARS

The bitterest tears shed over graves are for words left unsaid and deeds left undone.

Harriet Beecher Stowe

TEENAGERS

It never occurs to teenagers that someday they will know as little as their parents.

Why can't life's problems hit us when we're seventeen and know everything?

A.C. Jolly

In the 1940s a survey listed the top seven discipline problems in public schools: talking, chewing gum, making noise, running in the halls, getting out of line, wearing improper clothes, and not putting paper in wastebaskets. A more recent survey lists these top seven: drug abuse, alcohol abuse, pregnancy, suicide, rape, robbery, and assault. (Arson, gang warfare, and venereal disease are also-rans.)

George F. Will

TELEVISION

Television is now so desperately hungry for material that they're scraping the top of the barrel.

Gore Vidal

TEMPER

We must interpret a bad temper as a sign of inferiority.

Alfred Adler

Men lose their tempers in defending their taste.

Ralph Waldo Emerson

TEMPTATION

Temptation is a part of life. No one is immune—at any age. For temptation is present wherever there is a choice to be made, not only between good and evil, but also between a higher and lower good. For some, it may be a temptation to misuse their gifts, to seek a worthy aim by unworthy means, to lower their ideal to win favor with the electorate, or with their companions and associates.

Ernest Trice Thompson

Some temptations come to the industrious, but all temptations attack the idle.

Charles Haddon Spurgeon

TENACITY

Let me tell you the secret that has led me to my goal: my strength lies solely in my tenacity.

Louis Pasteur

The race is not always to the swift, but to those who keep on running.

TERM LIMITS

Congressional terms should be . . . ten to twenty with no possibility of parole.

Walt Handelsman

THANKFULNESS

If you can't be thankful for what you receive,
be thankful for what you escape.

Who does not thank for little will not
thank for much.

A thankful heart is not only the greatest virtue,
but the parent of all other virtues.

Cicero

If the only prayer you say in your whole life is
"Thank you," that would suffice.

Meister Eckhart

THEOLOGICAL ATTITUDE

Most of us retain enough of the theological attitude
to think that we are little gods.

Oliver Wendell Holmes Jr.

THEORY

A little experience often upsets a
lot of theory.

Cadman

THIEF

Set a thief to catch a thief.

THINGS

The best things in life aren't things.

Art Buchwald

THINKING

Crises and deadlocks when they occur have at least this advantage, that they force us to think.

Jawaharlal Nehru

As a man thinketh in his heart, so is he.

Proverbs 23:7

THOUGHTS

Our best friends and our worst enemies are our thoughts. A thought can do us more good than a doctor or a banker or a faithful friend. It can also do us more harm than a brick.

Dr. Frank Crane

If we were all to be judged by our thoughts, the hills would be swarming with outlaws.

Johann Sigurjonsson

If we are not responsible for the thoughts that pass our doors, we are at least responsible for those we admit and entertain.

Charles B. Newcomb

Be careful of your thoughts; they may become words at any moment.

Ira Gassen

THREADS

Chains do not hold a marriage together. It is threads, hundreds of tiny threads, which sew people together through the years.

Simone Signoret

TIGER

Some days you tame the tiger. And some days the tiger has you for lunch.

Tug McGraw

TIME

Time is an equal opportunity employer. Each human being has exactly the same number of hours and minutes every day. Rich people can't buy more hours. Scientists can't invent new minutes. And you can't save time to spend it on another day. Even so, time is amazingly fair and forgiving. No matter how much time you've wasted in the past, you still have an entire tomorrow. Success depends upon using it wisely—by planning and setting priorities.

Denis Waitely

Much may be done in those little shreds and patches of time which every day produces, and which most men throw away.

Charles Caleb Colton

Time is like a river of fleeting events, and its current is strong; as soon as something comes into sight, it is swept past us, and something else takes its place, and that too will be swept away.

Marcus Aurelius

Time is the wisest counselor of all.

Pericles

Dost thou love life? Then do not squander time, for that is the stuff life is made of.

Benjamin Franklin

Lost, yesterday, somewhere between sunrise
and sunset, two golden hours, each set with
sixty diamond minutes. No reward is
offered, for they are gone forever.

Horace Mann

If a person gives you his time, he can
give you no more precious gift.

Frank Tyger

Time is
Too slow for those who wait,
Too swift for those who fear,
Too long for those who grieve,
Too short for those who rejoice.
But for those who love, time is not.

Henry van Dyke

Pick my left pocket of its silver dime, but spare
the right—it holds my golden time!

Oliver Wendell Holmes

I resolve to live with all my might while I
do live. I resolve never to lose one moment of
time and to improve my use of time in
the most profitable way I possibly can. I
resolve never to do anything I wouldn't do,
if it were the last hour of my life.

Jonathan Edwards

TODAY

Live each day as you would climb a mountain. An occasional glance toward the summit keeps the goal in mind, but many beautiful scenes are to be observed from each new vantage point. So climb slowly, enjoying each passing moment; and then the view from the summit will serve a more rewarding climax for your journey.

Fulton J. Sheen

It is difficult to live in the present, ridiculous to live in the future and impossible to live in the past.

Jim Bishop

The days come and go like muffled and veiled figures sent from a distant friendly party, but they say nothing, and if we do not use the gifts they bring, they carry them as silently away.

Ralph Waldo Emerson

Enjoy today and don't waste it grieving over a bad yesterday—tomorrow may be even worse.

Do not look back on happiness, or dream of it in the future. You are only sure of today; do not let yourself be cheated out of it.

Henry Ward Beecher

Any idiot can face a crisis—it's day to day living that wears you out.

Anton Chekhov

The past, the present and the future are really one: they are today.

Harriet Beecher Stowe

TOES

Notice on wall in office of Admiral Arleigh A. Burke, Chief of Naval Operations: "When you're trying to get something done, don't worry too much about stepping on someone else's toes. Nobody gets his toes stepped on unless he is standing still or sitting down on the job."

TOLERANT

Nothing makes you more tolerant of a neighbor's noisy party than being there.

Franklin P. Jones

TOMORROW

Tomorrow is the most important thing in life. It comes to us at midnight very clean. It's perfect when it arrives, and it puts itself in our hands, and hopes we've learned something from yesterday.

John Wayne

TONGUE

Teach thy tongue to say "I do not know."

Maimonides

TOUPEE

His toupee makes him look twenty years sillier.

Bill Dana

TOWN

The town was so small it had only one yellow page.

Orson Bean

TRANQUILITY

Great tranquility of heart is his who cares for neither praise nor blame.

Thomas à Kempis

TREASON

Is there not some chosen curse, some hidden thunder in the stores of heaven, red with uncommon wrath, to blast the man who owes his greatness to his country's ruin!

Joseph Addison

TREE

He that plants a tree plants for posterity.

TRIALS

We are always in the forge, or on the anvil; by trials God is shaping us for higher things.

Henry Ward Beecher

The gem cannot be polished without friction, nor man perfected without trials.

All sunshine makes the desert.

It is not until we have passed through the furnace that we are made to know how much dross there is in our composition.

Charles Caleb Colton

I asked God for strength, that I might achieve—I was made weak, that I might learn humbly to obey.

TRIBULATION

There is no man in this world without some manner of tribulation or anguish, though he be king or pope.

Thomas à Kempis

TROUBLE

If winter comes, can spring be far behind?

Percy Bysshe Shelley

It is a painful thing to look at your own trouble and know that you yourself, and no one else, had made it.

Sophocles

Man is born unto trouble, as the sparks fly upward.

Job 5:7

No one would have crossed the ocean if he could have gotten off the ship in the storm.

Charles F. Kettering

Trouble creates a capacity to handle it.

Oliver Wendell Holmes Jr.

It never rains but it pours.

Trouble brings experience and experience brings wisdom.

He who fumes at his quandaries becomes their victim.

David Seabury

Troubles, like babies, grow larger by nursing.

Caroline Holland

Trouble is the thing that strong men grow by. Met in the right way, it is a sure-fire means of putting iron into the victim's will and making him a tougher man to down forever after.

H. Bertram Lewis

TRUST

I know God will not give me anything I can't handle. I just wish that He didn't trust me so much.

Mother Teresa

You may be deceived if you trust too much, but you will live in torment if you don't trust enough.

Frank Crane

No matter what may be the test,
God will take care of you;
Lean, weary one, upon His breast,
God will take care of you.

C.D. Martin

Blessed is the man that trusteth in the LORD,
and whose hope the LORD is.

Jeremiah 17:7

TRUTH

Everyone wishes to have truth on his side,
but not everyone wishes to be on
the side of truth.

Richard Whately

The truth is incontrovertible: malice may
attack it, ignorance may deride it,
but in the end, there it is.

Winston Churchill

And in the end, through the long ages of our
quest for light, it will be found that truth is still
mightier than the sword.

Douglas MacArthur

Truth has no special time of its own. Its
hour is now—always.

Albert Schweitzer

Truth is more of a stranger than fiction.

Mark Twain

Let the people know the truth and the country is safe.

Abraham Lincoln

Let my name stand among those who are willing to bear ridicule and reproach for the truth's sake, and so earn some right to rejoice when the victory is won.

Louisa May Alcott

Truth is tough. It will not break, like a bubble, at a touch. Nay, you may kick it about all day, and it will be round and full at evening.

Oliver Wendell Holmes

It is easier to perceive error than to find truth, for the former lies on the surface and is easily seen, while the latter lies in the depth, where few are willing to search for it.

Johann Wolfgang von Goethe

Seize upon truth, wherever it is found, amongst your friends, amongst your foes, on Christian or on heathen ground; the flower's divine where'er it grows.

Isaac Watts

I like better for one to say some foolish thing upon important matters than to be silent. That becomes the subject of discussion and dispute, and the truth is discovered.

Denis Diderot

Half the misery in the world comes of want of courage to speak and to hear the truth plainly, and in a spirit of love.

Harriet Beecher Stowe

Have patience awhile; slanders are not long-lived.
Truth is the child of time; ere long she shall
appear to vindicate thee.

Immanuel Kant

Truth is always consistent with itself, and needs
nothing to help it out; it is always near at hand,
sits upon our lips, and is ready to drop out before
we are aware; a lie is troublesome, and sets a
man's invention upon the rack, and one trick
needs a great many more to make it good. It is
like building upon a false foundation, which
continually stands in need of props to shore it up,
and proves at last more chargeable than to have
raised a substantial building at first upon a true
and solid foundation.

Joseph Addison

TRUTHFULNESS

Truthfulness is a corner-stone in character, and if it
be not firmly laid in youth, there will ever after be
a weak spot in the foundation.

Jefferson Davis

TRUE RELIGION

While just government protects all in their religious
rites, true religion affords government its
surest support.

George Washington

TRY

The men who try to do something and fail are infinitely better than those who try to do nothing and succeed.

Lloyd Jones

TYRANNY

There is a secret pride in every human heart that revolts at tyranny. You may order and drive an individual, but you cannot make him respect you.

William Hazlitt

UNCERTAINTY

Without measureless and perpetual uncertainty
the drama of human life would be destroyed.

Winston Churchill

UNCOMFORTABLE

Those people who are uncomfortable in
themselves are disagreeable to others.

William Hazlitt

UNDERSTANDING

Be kind, for everyone you meet is
fighting a hard battle.

Philo

Nothing in life is to be feared. It is only
to be understood.

Marie Curie

With different persons, we may be quite different
individuals. We cling, however, to the illusion
that we remain identical for all persons
and every situation.

Luigi Pirandello

UNEMPLOYED

The thing that really worries business today is the great number of people still on their payroll who are unemployed.

UNHAPPINESS

Much unhappiness results from our inability to remember the nice things that happen to us.

W.N. Rieger

There is nothing in the world so much admired as a man who knows how to bear unhappiness with courage.

Seneca

The most unhappy of all men is he who believes himself to be so.

David Hume

UNIONISM

Unionism seldom, if ever, uses such power as it has to insure better work; almost always it devotes a large part of that power to safeguarding bad work.

H.L. Mencken

UNKNOWN

Many live in dread of what is coming. Why should we? The unknown puts adventure into life. . . . The unexpected around the corner gives a sense of anticipation and surprise. Thank God for the unknown future.

E. Stanley Jones

UNSKILLED LABOR

Don't condescend to unskilled labor. Try it for a half a day first.

Brooks Atkinson

VACATION

Vacation: A period of travel and relaxation when you take twice the clothes you need, and half the money.

VALUE

The way to love anything is to realize that it may be lost.

G.K. Chesterton

The harder the conflict, the more glorious the triumph. What we obtain too cheaply, we esteem too lightly; 'tis dearness only that gives everything its value.

Thomas Paine

Try not to become a man of success but rather try to become a man of value.

Albert Einstein

Men must be decided on what they will not do, and then they are able to act with vigor in what they ought to do.

Mencius

VANITY

Of all our infirmities, vanity is the dearest to us; a man will starve his other vices to keep that alive.

Benjamin Franklin

There are no grades of vanity, there are only grades of ability in concealing it.

Mark Twain

The only cure for vanity is laughter, and the only fault that's laughable is vanity.

Henri Bergson

VARIETY

Change of pasture makes fat calves.

VENGEANCE

Nothing is more costly, nothing is more sterile, than vengeance.

Winston Churchill

No man ever did a designed injury to another, but at the same time he did a greater to himself.

Lord Kames

VICE

Every vice has its excuse ready.

Publilius Syrus

Search others for their virtues, thy
self for thy vices.

Benjamin Franklin

VIEWPOINT

The hues of the opal, the light of the diamond, are
not to be seen if the eye is too near.

Ralph Waldo Emerson

VILLAGE IDIOT

It was such a small town we didn't even have a
village idiot. We had to take turns.

Billy Holliday

VILLAIN

One may smile, and smile, and be a villain.

William Shakespeare

VIRTUE

Order your soul; reduce your wants; live in
charity; associate in Christian community;
obey the laws; trust in Providence.

Saint Augustine

Virtue, though in rags, will keep me warm.

John Dryden

We are apt to mistake our vocation by looking out
of the way for occasions to exercise great and
rare virtues, and by stepping over the ordinary
ones that lie directly in the road before us.

Hannah More

VISA CARD

I just recently had my Visa card stolen. . . . Right now it's everywhere I want to be.

Scott Wood

VISION

Vision is the art of seeing things invisible.

Jonathan Swift

VOCABULARY

I used to think I was poor. Then they told me I wasn't poor, I was needy. Then they told me it was self-defeating to think of myself as needy, that I was culturally deprived. Then they told me deprived was a bad image, that I was underprivileged. Then they told me underprivileged was overused, that I was disadvantaged. I still don't have a dime, but I do have a great vocabulary.

Jules Feiffer

VOTE

Always vote for principle, though you may vote alone, and you may cherish the sweetest reflection that your vote is never lost.

John Quincy Adams

WAGE

Give the labourer his wage before his perspiration be dry.

Muhammad

WALKING

Thoughts come clearly while one walks.

Thomas Mann

WAR

It is fatal to enter any war without the will to win it.

Douglas MacArthur

WARRIORS

The strongest of all warriors are these two: time and patience.

Leo Tolstoy

WEAKNESS

If thou wouldst conquer thy weakness thou must never gratify it. No man is compelled to evil; only his consent makes it his. It is no sin to be tempted; it is to yield and be overcome.

William Penn

WEALTH

Wealth unused might as well not exist.

Aesop

WEEP

It is better to weep with wise men than to laugh with fools.

WHINE

Boys, this is only a game. But it's like life in that you will be dealt some bad hands. Take each hand, good or bad, and don't whine and complain, but play it out. If you're men enough to do that, God will help and you will come out well.

Dwight D. Eisenhower's mother

WIFE

A good wife makes a good husband.

WILL

People do not lack strength; they lack will.

Victor Hugo

If you have the will to win, you have achieved half your success. If you don't, you have achieved half your failure.

David Ambrose

WISDOM

All human wisdom is summed up in two words: wait and hope.

Alexandre Dumas

Nine-tenths of wisdom consists in being wise in time.

Theodore Roosevelt

There is a piece of fortune in misfortune.

The silent person is often worth listening to.

Wisdom is the reward you get for a lifetime of listening when you'd have preferred to talk.

Doug Larson

One man's word is no man's word; we should quietly hear both sides.

Johann Wolfgang von Goethe

He that stumbles twice over one stone
deserves to break his shins.

When you go to buy, don't show your silver.

Tell nothing to thy friend that thine enemy
may not know.

WISH

Nothing is so easy as to deceive one's self; for
what we wish, that we readily believe.

Demosthenes

A man will sometimes devote all his life to the
development of one part of his
body—the wishbone.

Robert Lee Frost

The reason some men do not succeed is
because their wishbone is where their
backbone ought to be.

WIT

Wit makes its own welcome, and levels all
distinctions. No dignity, no learning, no force of
character, can make any stand against good wit.

Ralph Waldo Emerson

Wit is a sword; it is meant to make people feel
the point as well as see it.

G.K. Chesterton

WITNESS

Every week our preacher tells us to go out and "witness" to others. But nothing strikes more fear in my heart than having to share my faith with a complete stranger. It's gotten so bad I've enrolled in a Witness Relocation Program.

Robert G. Lee

WOMAN

I kissed my first woman and smoked my first cigarette on the same day; I have never had time for tobacco since.

Arturo Toscanini

WONDER

When I was young, my parents told me what to do; now that I am old, my children tell me what to do. I wonder when I will be able to do what I want to do.

The world will never starve for want of wonders, but for want of wonder.

Gilbert K. Chesterton

As knowledge increases, wonder deepens.

Charles Morgan

WORDS

You never know when a moment and a few sincere words can have an impact on a life.

Zig Ziglar

My words fly up, my thoughts
remain below; Words without thoughts
never to heaven go.

William Shakespeare

Words that come from the heart enter the heart.

If you your lips would keep from slips,
Five things observe with care;
To whom you speak, of whom you speak,
And how, and when, and where.

William Edward Norris

One great use of words is to hide our thoughts.

Voltaire

The more articulate one is,
the more dangerous words become.

Mary Sarton

WORK

The right way to kill time is to work it to death.

R.G. LeTourneau

There may be luck in getting a good job—
but there's no luck in keeping it.

Jonathan Ogden Armour

I never knew an early-rising, hard-working, prudent
man, careful of his earnings, and strictly honest,
who complained of bad luck. A good character,
good habits, and iron industry are impregnable to
the assaults of all the ill-luck that fools ever
dreamed of.

Joseph Addison

Footprints on the sands of time are not made by sitting down.

What the country needs is dirtier fingernails and cleaner minds.

Will Rogers

Work is the meat of life, pleasure the dessert.

Bertie Charles Forbes

I believe in work, hard work, and long hours of work. Men do not break down from overwork, but from worry and dissipation.

Charles Evans Hughes

Give me a man who sings at his work.

Thomas Carlyle

Men seldom die of hard work; activity is God's medicine. The highest genius is willingness and ability to do hard work. Any other conception of genius makes it a doubtful, if not a dangerous possession.

Robert Stuart MacArthur

For anything worth having one must pay the price; and the price is always work, patience, love, self-sacrifice.

John Burroughs

Find your place and hold it: find your work and do it. And put everything you've got into it.

Edward William Bok

A truly American sentiment recognizes the dignity of labor and the fact that honor lies in honest toil.

Grover Cleveland

Go and wake up your luck.

Do not expect a "well done" if you have
not done well.

D. James Kennedy

If you are poor, work. If you are rich, work.
If you are burdened with seemingly unfair
responsibilities, work. When men are rightly
occupied, their amusement grows out of their
work, as the color-petals
out of a fruitful flower.

John Ruskin

Better wear out shoes than sheets.

He that would have fruit must climb the tree.

Thomas Fuller

Everything considered, work is less boring
than amusing oneself.

Charles Baudelaire

Work is the best method devised for killing time.

William Feather

I do not know anyone who has gotten to the top
without hard work. That is the recipe.

Margaret Thatcher

If I were to suggest a general rule for happiness,
I would say "Work a little harder; work a
little longer; work!"

Frederick H. Ecker

Nothing is really work unless you would rather be doing something else.

James Matthew Barrie

Too many people quit looking for work when they find a job.

Labor is man's greatest function. He is nothing, he can do nothing he can achieve nothing, he can fulfill nothing, without working.

Orville Dewey

WORKING OUT

I'm not into working out. My philosophy: No pain, no pain.

Carol Leifer

WORRY

Worry is a futile thing, it's somewhat like a rocking chair, Although it keeps you occupied, it doesn't get you anywhere.

There is nothing so wretched or foolish as to anticipate misfortunes. What madness is it in expecting evil before it arrives?

Marcus Annaeus Seneca

Do not worry; eat three square meals a day; say your prayers; be courteous to your creditors; keep your digestion good; exercise; go slow and easy. Maybe there are other things your special case requires to make you happy; but, my friend, these I reckon will give you a good lift.

Abraham Lincoln

How much pain they have cost us, the evils which have never happened.

Thomas Jefferson

The reason why worry kills more people than work is that more people worry than work.

Robert Frost

Worry never climbed a hill,
worry never paid a bill,
Worry never dried a tear,
worry never calmed a fear,
Worry never darned a heel,
worry never cooked a meal,
It never led a horse to water,
nor ever did a thing it "oughter."

Which of you by taking thought can add one cubit unto his stature?

Matthew 6:27

Every evening I turn worries over to God. He's going to be up all night anyway.

Mary C. Crowley

Don't tell me that worry doesn't do any good. I
know better. The things I worry about
don't happen.

WORTH

Now that it's all over, what did you really do yesterday that's worth mentioning?

Coleman Cox

There is no readier way for a man to bring his
own worth into question, than by endeavoring to
detract from the worth of other men.

John Tillotson

We never know the worth of water
till the well is dry.

WORTHWHILE

Show me someone who has done something
worthwhile, and I'll show you someone who has
overcome adversity.

Lou Holtz

WRATH

When wrath speaks, wisdom veils her face.

WRITING

The writer must be willing, above everything else,
to take chances, to risk making a fool of himself—
or even to risk revealing the fact that he is a fool.

Jessamyn West

About the most originality that any writer can hope to achieve honestly is to steal with good judgment.

Josh Billings

A painter can hang his pictures, but a writer can only hang himself.

Edward Dahlberg

A drop of ink may make a million think.

Lord Byron

The profession of book writing makes horse racing seem like a solid, stable business.

John Steinbeck

When something can be read without effort, great effort has gone into its writing.

Enrique Jardiel Poncela

Your manuscript is both good and original, but the part that is good is not origianl, and the part that is original is not good.

Samuel Johnson

Most people won't realize that writing is a craft. You have to take your apprenticeship in it like anything else.

Katherine Anne Porter

WRONG

The man who says "I may be wrong, but . . ." does not believe there can be any such possibility.

Frank McKinney (Kin) Hubbard

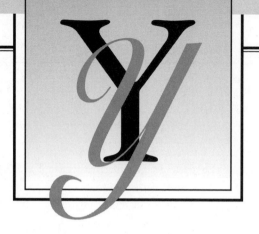

YOUTH

It is better to be a young June-bug
than an old bird of paradise.

Mark Twain

Youth is a wonderful thing: what a
crime to waste it on children.

George Bernard Shaw

Oh, this age! How tasteless
and illbred it is!

Catullus

It is not possible for civilization to
flow backwards while there is
youth in the world.

Helen Keller

Youth comes but once in a lifetime.

Henry Wadsworth Longfellow

Youth is not entirely a time of life; it is a state of mind. Nobody grows old by merely living a number of years. People grow old by deserting their ideals. You are as young as your faith, as old as your doubt; as young as your self-confidence, as old as your fear; as young as your hope, as old as your despair.

Douglas MacArthur

Youth is that period when a young boy knows everything but how to make a living.

Carey Williams

The youth of a nation are the trustees of posterity.

Benjamin Disraeli

Don't laugh at a youth for his affectations; he is only trying on one face after another to find his own.

Logan Pearsall Smith

I love the acquaintance of young people, because, in the first place, I don't like to think myself growing old. In the next place, young acquaintances must last longest, if they do last; and then young men have more virtue than old men; they have more generous sentiments in every respect.

Samuel Johnson

The denunciation of the young is a necessary part of the hygiene of older people, and greatly assists the circulation of their blood.

Logan Pearsall Smith

ZEAL

Most great men and women are not
perfectly rounded in their personalities,
but are instead people whose one driving
enthusiasm is so great it makes
their faults seem insignificant.

Charles A. Cerami

Zeal is like fire; it needs both
feeding and watching.